⊕ MULTI-CENTRE ⊕
WOODTURNING

⊕ **MULTI-CENTRE** ⊕
WOODTURNING

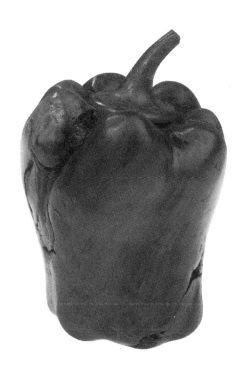

RAY HOPPER

GUILD OF MASTER CRAFTSMAN PUBLICATIONS LTD

First Published in 1992 by
Guild of Master Craftsman Publications Ltd,
Castle Place, 166 High Street,
Lewes, East Sussex BN7 1XU

Reprinted 1993, 1994

© Ray Hopper 1992

ISBN 0 946819 35 1

Illustrations © Geoff Ford 1992

Photography © Steve Whiting 1992

Designed by Fineline Studios

Printed in Great Britain by Alden Press Ltd,
Oxford

Dedication

To Kathy, for her continuing support and encouragement

Acknowledgements

With thanks to the following:

Professor Dr D. Ellegiers, who gave me the opportunity to demonstrate woodturning in the schools and colleges of Belgium, which gave me an insight into their very fine skills in crafting wood;

John Ambrose, President of the Ely Guild of Woodturners, for introducing me to the Guild and thus stimulating my woodturning;

Ely Guild of Woodturners members Ken Howard, for the idea for the laminated handle in Chapter 4, Derek Phillips, for the idea for the egg timer in Chapter 6, and Philip Irons, for the idea for the caddy spoons in Chapter 27;

Brian O'Kane of Herts Tree Care for the photographs of his arboretum, and for supplying the burrs.

John Camp, for his advice on fire prevention.

Steve Whiting, for taking such excellent photography in the somewhat cramped conditions of my workshop.

Geoff Ford, for his enthusiastic interpretation of the drawings.

The staff at Guild of Master Craftsman Publications, for their teamwork in producing this book.

Contents

Foreword

Woodturning is an art, one of the applied arts, with a great tradition. The basis of art includes technical expertise, intellectual activity, brainwork and creativity; but without technical expertise, no further step is possible. For this reason alone, technical books like Ray Hopper's are all-important. And good books on woodturning techniques are very rare: to my knowledge there is no other book on this particular aspect of woodturning – multi-centre turning.

Some of the most creative possibilities in woodworking lie in woodturning, marquetry and woodcarving. But woodturning tops them all: it is fairly easy to learn the basic techniques, the investment is moderate, blanks can be found for free in the woods, and creativity is unlimited.

In the realm of furniture, woodturning has always been important: columns, chair- and tablelegs, all kinds of decorations were turned, and they embellished a piece of furniture.

Woodturning makes a piece of furniture flowing, smarter, more aesthetic, more pleasant, because woodturning means details. Woodturning makes a piece of furniture better value for money, and it is again beginning to play a role in modern furniture design.

In education, woodturning could be a welcome addition to school syllabuses, as it is easy to learn and the results are immediate and consequently very motivating; and lack of motivation is the frequent lament of teachers.

Woodturning shows wood to its best advantage, and it is creative, again something necessary in life itself: nothing is more gratifying than creating something beautiful, something that will live on. There are hundreds of possible creative models, for bowls, platters, boxes, chandeliers, etc., and some are real works of art. It is in this field of woodturning that one feels completely free; it is here that creativity has no bounds, no links to utility, and that is probably a way to art, to real art.

Emeritus Professor Dr D Ellegiers
Gavere-Vurste, Belgium, June 1992

Author's Note

Before attempting multi-centre woodturning, the reader should at least be fully competent in using woodturning tools; *Woodturning: A Foundation Course* by Keith Rowley (GMC Publications, 1990) shows the correct way to use and sharpen tools, gives the basic laws and practices of woodturning, and sets a standard to be reached.

Introduction

Why I Turn Wood

I have worked with wood in its many disciplines since I left school, and hope to for many years to come. My first job was in a joiners' shop, mixing glue, sweeping up the wood shavings and assisting the joiners; the foreman told me I would only have to do this for six months, and I would then have a bench of my own. It seemed more like six years. When I finally got my bench, I was allowed to go on a City and Guilds course for carpentry and joinery one day a week - but lost that day's pay.

I then tried working for a small firm that made Queen Anne reproduction furniture, which was veneered with burr walnut veneers; however, a lot of the work was done by machine, and I was still losing pay to pass my exam, so I joined another company and was contracted to construct 40ft queen post roof trusses and erect them in the London docks. This gave me experience in heavy carpentry - all the joints were cut by hand - and I then worked in the West End of London as a shopfitter before a three-month spell making coffins from solid elm boards.

At another time I worked, with 40 other maintenance carpenters, for a company which manufactured products from coal. Everything was made or repaired by hand in the large carpenters' shop: this ranged from heavy wooden railway carriage chassis made from green oak to office and laboratory furniture. There was only one machine in the workshop, a large coal gas-driven circular saw: a massive piston drove round an 8ft diameter flywheel, firing only once every one or two seconds. It was started first thing in the morning and left to run all day. The sawyer, a sturdy man with a droopy moustache stained from chewing betelnut tobacco, only had to pull a lever to move a 4in wide leather belt from the free-running pulley to the drive pulley to put the saw in motion. Whatever depth of timber was pushed through, the machine never slowed. I can see him now, pushing large beams of timber through on this saw, with his thumbs only an inch away from either side of the revolving blade. The simplicity of this machine, with its few moving parts, intrigued me.

Finally, after a short time in the building trade I spent over 30 years as a foreman in a woodworking shop and allied trades.

I have respected wood, worked out with it in all weathers, become frustrated with it and

Fig 1.1 My metal-spinning lathe.

cursed it. Woodturning I have always enjoyed: at school I planed the corners off a piece of wood to put in the lathe, but my turn to use the lathe and get the feel of woodturning tools never came. As soon as I could, I bought an old metal-spinning lathe (*see* Fig 1.1), and taught myself to turn tool handles and bowls from elm offcuts from the coffin workshop.

This was in the late 1940s; since then, woodturning in Britain has progressed dramatically. I am still fascinated by the lathe, as in all my woodworking experience it is the only machine that will do all the work while I am still in control, guiding the turning tool wherever I wish. The lathe does the work from the very beginning - I recently put a 2ft length of 6in square timber between centres on a woodturning lathe and gently but firmly fed the roughing gouge in to remove the corners - to the end, even waxing and polishing.

Woodturning can be a lonely hobby; through attending seminars and being an active member of the Ely Guild of Woodturners, I have learned a lot and have been stimulated to experiment and develop the ideas and methods in this book. Others in the Guild have since developed particular aspects of multi-centre turning, and the projects here suggest how the reader can do the same.

Quality of Workmanship

In my opinion, a great deal of turned work is well made but is spoilt by not spending time and a little effort on obtaining a good finish: detailed sections such as mouldings and corners should be left crisp and not rounded over with sandpaper, and flat surfaces should be perfectly smooth, any marks left by turning tools having been removed. The finish is so important – it is the first thing you notice.

I recently noticed some wooden bowls in a shop window near the premises of the publishers of this book; the bowls were made from 4in thick x 10in diameter teak, and the price was less than that of a bowl blank of comparative size, but the finish – what a letdown! The bowls had been imported from South-East Asia, and the shipping costs must have been more economical than for 4in thick planks of teak in Britain, but woodturning's good name could be at risk if too much shoddy work is presented.

Whatever the design or the type of wood used, always aim for a good finish: look at the wood, branch, burr or log, and visualize what you intend to make, but visualize it as a high-quality article with a perfect finish. Then see how close you can get to that ideal.

Every woodturner has a percentage of work that has not come up to standard; it may

be through no fault of his or her own – the fault may be in the wood or in trying to make a thin or delicate object. If I am disappointed with a bowl made from a piece of wood selected for its unusual grain, I do not put it on a shelf and wish it had turned out better. I jump on it and then put it in the waste box and carry on with the next project.

The Future

I have a great respect for the early craftsmen and their tools; being fortunate enough to have been taught by good craftsmen, I have endeavoured to pass on their knowledge to the apprentices I have trained. In this age of electronic gadgetry, it is important to keep the old crafts and skills alive, and the revival and increase of interest in woodturning could be developed and expanded. For instance, turned wood could be used more on individual pieces of furniture, while woodcarving on turned wood could be redeveloped. Architects could easily utilize the re-emerging woodturning arts: turned work could be effectively used in buildings, from reception areas to the finials on the rooftops.

It must benefit society to see the old skills being revived, and to give younger generations encouragement and the chance to use their hands to develop these skills. Through this, they will have the satisfaction of creation and the ability to appreciate the difference between a plastic bowl and a wooden bowl they have designed and made.

CHAPTER 2

Safety

In my younger days I took many shortcuts and risks, and I am fortunate never to have had a serious accident, but I have seen many accidents happen with wood and woodworking machinery. Most would not have occurred had a few simple rules been followed; for the projects in this book, always check that the work is securely mounted between centres, and that the lathe speed is slower rather than faster for the work you are turning. An accident does not take very long to happen, but the results can be permanent.

Having started work with joiners who took a great pride in their tools and their work, and having also built up my own tool kit, I tended to resist some of the changes in working practice that came about over the subsequent years; some were necessary, and some were put down to progress. But when some new safety regulations came into force, I became what was known as a 'prejudiced woodworker', and among other things resisted wearing the then uncomfortable, heavy dustmasks.

Since those days, I have come to realize how important it is to look after one's own health and safety. With today's technology and developments, there are more effective ways of

protecting the woodworker and woodturner, and, possibly just as importantly, the newer safety equipment is comfortable to wear (*see* below).

There are some situations in industry where it is almost impossible to have an accident: in a car factory, for example, two or three men may be placing sheets of metal in a large press forming car sections. This machine is designed to operate only if each worker has both hands on the separate start buttons, which are at a distance away from the press. Woodturners do not have this sort of built-in protection; it is not practical to fit guards on woodturning lathes, so it is up to each individual to follow the set rules to minimize the chance of an accident.

Don't work when you are tired; stay alert and listen to sounds on the lathe that could be a warning of danger. It all boils down to common sense.

Protective Clothing

Do not switch your lathe on until after you have put on a face shield. It takes little effort, but it could save your sight. It also allows you to see what you are doing clearly, without having to partly close your eyes to avoid woodshavings flying off the lathe; in addition, it prevents some of the particles of dust entering your respiratory system.

Even if your workshop is fitted with a dust-extraction system, it is advisable to wear a nose and mouth mask, especially if you are turning some of the exotic woods. For instance, it is known that African boxwood can cause cancer over a period of time. There is an extensive list of known harmful woods, but what may not be apparent are the long-term effects of some of the more recent woods to have appeared on the market. Wood dust in general is harmful – it is the fine dust that cannot be seen that can be a health hazard.

My faceguard is fitted with a powered respirator: it is important to use one of the types available, either a facemask or combined visor and filter system, so that the air is filtered

Fig 2.1 Dustmask and face shield with electric fan attachment.

before it reaches your respiratory system. It will also keep shavings and dust out of the hair, and should be comfortable to wear.

The dustmask and face shield I now use has a lightweight filter unit fitting on to a belt around my waist; this houses a small electric fan driven by a rechargeable battery (*see* Fig 2.1). The filtered air is piped to the top of the face shield, and cool air is then gently blown over the face. For me, the most important feature is the cloth surround, which fits comfortably around my face and chin and pressurises the clean air in the face shield: the same system is used in the large areas, used for assembling satellites and space vehicles, that I have helped construct. The fact that these areas are pressurised prevents even the finest particles of dust from entering the area.

If you wear clothing with long sleeves, make sure these are fastened at the wrist: you can never afford to have flapping cuffs or sleeves while woodturning. It is a good idea to wear industrial gloves when turning some of the projects in this book, as these reduce the chances of having your knuckles rapped. I wear shoes with steel toecaps; although this is not a must for woodturners, they are comfortable to wear and have saved me from bruised or possibly broken toes when I have dropped the odd heavy bowl blank or turning tool.

If your protective clothing is comfortable and your working environment is well thought-out, you will reduce the chances of accidents.

Setting Out Your Workshop

This section comes under safety, as it should be a major factor in planning where you work. Setting out a workshop means making good use of available space and placing your tools, safety gear and machines where you can easily and safely reach them.

The electrics and wiring of the workshop should be completed by a qualified electrician; it is then your responsibility to see that the system is used correctly. Electricity will serve you well, but if you abuse or neglect it, it can give you a shock or worse. Make regular visual checks of all leads and plugs for cuts and other damage, and if a fuse blows, find out why, and never replace it with a fuse of the incorrect amperage. Should any electrical equipment or wiring overheat, turn off the power until the fault has been located and put right.

An important requirement is a switch at each side of the lathe, so that you can cut off the power in an emergency. An **ECB electrical circuit-breaker** should be fitted into the electrical supply before it reaches the workshop, so the supply is automatically cut off should anything go wrong.

You will need good lighting positioned at both ends of the lathe, but not where it can be knocked out by a piece of wood flying off the lathe. If there is a source of natural light, place the lathe to take best advantage of it – natural light takes a lot of beating: you do not get as much shadow as with artificial light, and some artificial light produces a strobe effect. This is

Fig 2.2 My portable folding lathe, made of
plywood; note the clutch pedal. It is useful
in multi-centre woodturning to have the
facility to slow down or stop the lathe.

not very helpful when turning wood, as the frequency of the light combined with the lathe revolutions can be misleading, if not dangerous. This does not happen very often, but in certain circumstances a circular saw blade can appear to be revolving backwards. Multi-centre woodturning can also be a good subject for such an optical illusion; to illustrate this and to check the lighting in your workshop, stick a small piece of paper to the blade of a domestic electric fan. When the fan is switched on and off, the paper will sometimes appear to be stationary or revolving backwards.

One advantage of having woodturning as a hobby is that you do not need a great deal of space compared to some other branches of woodwork; for example, making even small items of furniture, where frames have to be glued together etc., or where the area has to be large enough to accommodate a circular saw.

All the projects in this book were made in my 8ft x 18ft greenhouse. I do not, however, recommend anyone to use a greenhouse for a workshop; the glass in mine is reinforced with wire, as well as being protected with plywood at points in line with anything that might fly off the lathe, and there is enough room for my three lathes, bandsaw, bench drill, twin grinding wheel, belt sander and small planing machine with 4in wide cutter.

The bench needs only to be wide enough to accommodate a bench drill stand and a grinding wheel unit. All woodturning tools can be sharpened on the grinding wheel (except the skew chisel, which is the only tool that needs a cutting edge finished on an oilstone), so the grinding wheel needs to be placed as near as safety allows to where you operate your lathe.

To use tools safely they need to be sharp. The angles for grinding your woodturning tools for multi-centre turning will be the same as the ones used for sharpening tools for true centre turning. Your grinding wheel should be no less than 150mm in diameter, and should preferably be 25mm wide. It is important to keep the grinding wheel surface flat; this can be achieved using conventional grinding wheel dressing tools. With multi-centre turning you will be using the bowl gouge and spindle gouge more, and the skew chisel less, than you would with true centre turning.

My most frequently used tools, i.e. turning tools, dividers, templates, chucks etc., hang in racks within easy reach. Wood shavings inevitably seem to settle everywhere, and I find it a good idea to fit as many cupboards and drawers as practicable to keep out the shavings and dust. If possible, arrange to have an exit at each end of your workshop, particularly if it is long and narrow – it is nice to know you have a bolt hole, even if you never have to use it.

Fire

There are three main fire hazards of which the woodturner should be aware:

1 Inflammable liquids Cellulose-based sealers and polishes, and methylated spirit-based polish are two of the most volatile. There may be a jar on a shelf containing white spirit, in which you wash brushes used for polyurethane – all inflammable liquids should be kept in a metal cabinet.

2 Electricity Even when all your equipment is correctly wired and in good condition, there are sparks coming off the armatures of electric drills and electric motors. Partial short circuit and insulation breakdown, or overloading, can all cause wiring to overheat and become a fire hazard. Also think about the heating in your workshop – be careful not to introduce another fire risk.

3 Wood shavings and dust Wood shavings are obviously inflammable, but wood dust can also explode, given the right conditions. Hardwood dust forms an inflammable cloud which will explode when ignited. A small explosion may disturb accumulations of dust and create a larger flammable cloud, which could in turn lead to a secondary explosion severe enough to destroy a workshop. The risk of this happening in your workshop may be small, but never forget that an accident can be the result of just such a combination of small risks. Drilling deep holes in table lamps, with the lathe going too fast or with the drill bit blunt, can cause heat and smouldering, then a draught from the work revolving in the lathe can fan the smouldering waste and create a fire. Sparks from a grinding wheel can also be a fire

hazard. Good housekeeping is all-important: it can reduce the fire risk and increase safety.

You may feel safe because you already have a fire extinguisher handy, but is it the right type?

A **red** extinguisher contains water, and this must not be used on electrical or flammable liquid fires.

A **cream-coloured** extinguisher contains foam, and this must not be used on electrical fires; it is not very effective on wood shavings.

A **green** extinguisher contains halon bcf, which is internationally agreed to be ozone-unfriendly.

A **blue** extinguisher contains a powder which is a general-purpose fire extinguisher and is correct for the woodturning workshop – but there is a catch: these extinguishers have a limited shelf life, so note the dates on the label. Refills can be purchased for modern extinguishers.

If you own one of the old **brass** extinguishers, this contains trichloroethylene, which is dangerous to the user. The best use for it is to remove tar or oil spots from clothes, and keep the brass canister as an ornament.

Finally, fix a NO SMOKING notice at the entrance to your workshop, and **make sure it is obeyed.**

Hints and Finishes

Hints

It can be seen from some of the photographs in this book that sometimes when the projects are revolving between centres, there is an area of solid wood and an area that looks blurred. This is particularly helpful when the blurred area has to be removed for the project.

A dark background will give a clearer definition of the blurred area, and I prop a

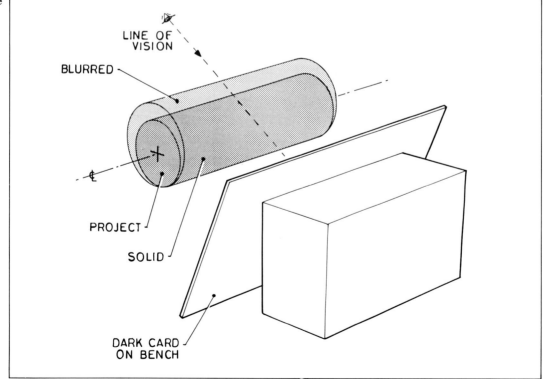

Fig 3.1 Line of vision through a project on the lathe.

LINE OF VISION

BLURRED

PROJECT

SOLID

DARK CARD ON BENCH

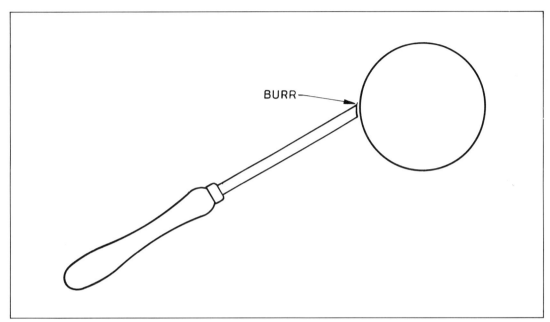

Fig 3.2
Sharpening
a scraper.

BURR

piece of black Formica on my lathe bench for this purpose — a piece of dark card, hardboard or plywood painted black will also serve. Fig 3.1 shows the line of vision through a project on the lathe on to a dark background.

There are also situations where blurred areas can be seen on faceplate turning, for example when turning the wings of the bowls in Chapter 29. Here one can see the cutting edge of the tool through the blurred area of the project; this is also very helpful when turning a project very thin, as one can see both the thickness of the wood to be retained and the thickness of the wood shaving being removed by the cutting edge.

Another way of marking positions to be cut can be seen in the photographs in Chapter 18: here the blurred areas have been marked with a thick felt marker pen. As will be seen, this method is used for a number of these projects.

Finishes

Finishes and finishing are personal matters for most woodturners; the most important thing is to get a good finish off the tool: as said before, sanding is no substitute! Many finishes are available from craft supply outlets: cellulose- and spirit-based sealers and polishes, hard and soft wax finishes, and a range of oil finishes. Let's start with the last cuts of the turning tool, which will prepare the work for the final finish.

On work turned between centres, a finish that will only need a fine grit paper before needing a sealer can be achieved with a sharp skew chisel. At this stage you may be using a skew, gouge or beading tool. In each case, firmly rest the bevel on the work and slowly lift the handle until you are making a very fine cut.

The scraper, of course, has a different action to other turning tools. It is a solid, flat-section tool sharpened on a grinding wheel to form an obtuse or short bevel. Sharpening the tool in this way forms a burr – *see* Fig 3.2. The scraper can give a very good finish, and it will remove tooling marks left by other tools, but keep a close watch on the work – the scraper can also pull out the end-grain fibres on some woods.

The Velcro sanding system is a very helpful innovation for woodturners. It is basically a replaceable sandpaper disc that fits on a pad; this pad is then placed in the chuck of a pistol-type electric drill or on a flexible drive unit. This system is ideal for faceplate work: bowls, platters, etc. You can use whatever grit suits the work: I normally use 150 grit and then 400 grit to finish. 60 grit, which can be handy for green timber bowls, is also available, as is 400 grit for superfine finishing.

A cellulose-based sander sealer can be used on softwoods to seal the grain: I use a half-and-half blend of beeswax and carnauba to get a good wax finish. Craftlac melamine gives a good finish on hardwoods: apply a thin film over the workpiece while the lathe is stationary – melamine does not raise the grain, and dries in minutes – then take a piece of 0000 grade steel wool and dip it into a soft paste wax. Start the lathe, apply the paste to the surface and then polish with a soft cloth.

Projects

Woodturning Tools for the Projects

There are four basic sections for woodturning tools: s**kew, gouge, parting and beading tool,** and **scraper**; and of course there are also large numbers of variations and sizes of these. In my experience, most woodturners have their own preferences as to which tool they use, and to which angle it is sharpened. Indeed, some make their own tools to suit a particular piece of work, as can be seen in some of these projects.

Because woodturning is such a personal thing, one can usually identify the work of other woodturners, as we all work in different ways and styles. It is for these reasons that I have only listed the tools used in some of the projects; it would otherwise be rather repetitive. Also, it is intended that most of the projects are ideas and methods to be experimented with, and with the variations of tools of the turner's own choosing.

Finally, do remember that woodturning at this level <u>is</u> potentially hazardous. It should not be attempted by anyone who has not already achieved a good standard of skill, and all safety precautions should be observed throughout.

Oval Tool Handles

Oval handles have important functions in the use of tools: you need an oval handle on a screwdriver to obtain maximum purchase when driving or removing screws; hammers, pickaxes etc., have oval handles so that they are correctly oriented for striking when gripped; some wood chisels are manufactured with oval handles so that the cutting edge will be in the correct plane when the tool is picked up. Oval-handled tools also provide better control and are less likely to roll off the workbench – for these reasons, I have made oval handles for some of my woodturning tools.

The tools needed will be: drill bit, roughing gouge, skew chisel, parting tool and scraper.

Almost any hardwood will be suitable for this project; the wood for a woodturning tool handle should be about 300mm x 50mm x 50mm, but this could be changed depending on the size of the blade. You will need a ferrule of

Fig 4.1 Cutting out the tang shape.

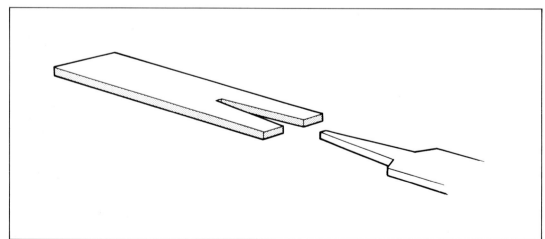

the right size for the handle: these can be purchased from most tool shops, but I prefer to cut mine from any suitable odd length of brass or copper pipe.

Method

Either a solid timber blank or a laminated section can be used.

Flat tang

The laminated section is built up as follows: first cut a piece of suitable wood 300mm x 50mm and the thickness of the tang. Place the tang on it, mark the shape and cut out (*see* Fig

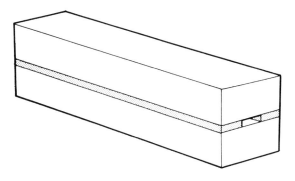

Fig 4.2 Making a laminated section.

4.1). Cut two more pieces of wood in a contrasting colour, about 23mm thick, and place one on each side as in Fig 4.2. Glue them together – a suitable glue for this purpose

Fig 4.3 Holes for receiving the spur wings.

would be Evo-stik Resin 'W' wood adhesive, or Unibond or Polybond.

You can turn a very attractive handle from this laminate, and it is also a chance to use thinner pieces of wood, thus saving larger sections for other projects. The blade tang can of course be inserted without fear of splitting the handle.

Fig 4.4 Shaping the headstock end.

Round tang

First drill a hole in one end of the blank to receive the tang of the blade; this will not be necessary for the glued version, as the hole for the tang has already been made. The hole can now be fitted over a revolving centre.

Make a saw cut in the other end of the wood to receive the spur wings on the drive

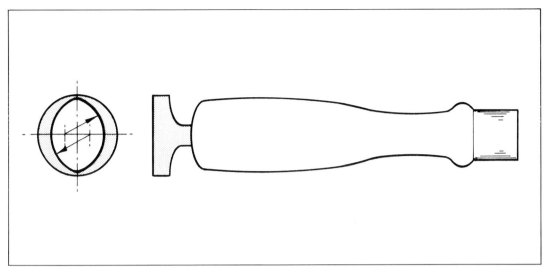

Fig 4.5 Suitable shape.

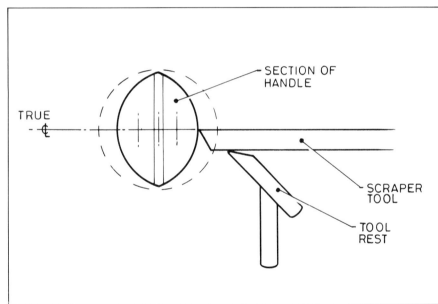

**Fig 4.6 The cutting edge
must be level with the line
between centres.**

spur that fits on the headstock. Drill three small holes in this cut to receive the spur point: one at centre, the other two 6mm each side of centre – *see* Fig 4.3.

Oval shaping

Place the wood between centres and turn down to a cylindrical shape with a roughing gouge. Turn the wood down to a diameter that the ferrule will fit over at the tailstock end. Tap the

ferrule on: this will help to stop the end of the handle splitting while the rest of the work is carried out. Start to shape the headstock end of the handle until it looks like that shown in Fig 4.4.

This is where you start the multi-centre turning. First put your face shield on, then move the workpiece from the true centre, replace it on to one of the off-centre marks and carefully feed in the gouge to remove a few shavings at the headstock end of the lathe. This will be the oval part of the handle. Now move the work to the remaining off-centre mark and remove the same amount of wood. Remount the work in either off-centre location and remove more wood, continuing until you have the suitable shape, which should look something like that in Fig 4.5. Now go back to the true centre mark and carefully finish shaping the handle.

Fig 4.7
A selection
of handles.

It can happen that the long axis of the oval shape does not run parallel with the slot prepared for the blade tang. To correct this, the cutting edge of the turning tool has to be level with the line between centres. This final cut is best achieved with a scraper – *see* Fig 4.6.

When a screwdriver blade is fitted to the handle, make sure the blade is parallel to the oval of the handle – Fig 4.7 shows various handles that have been turned.

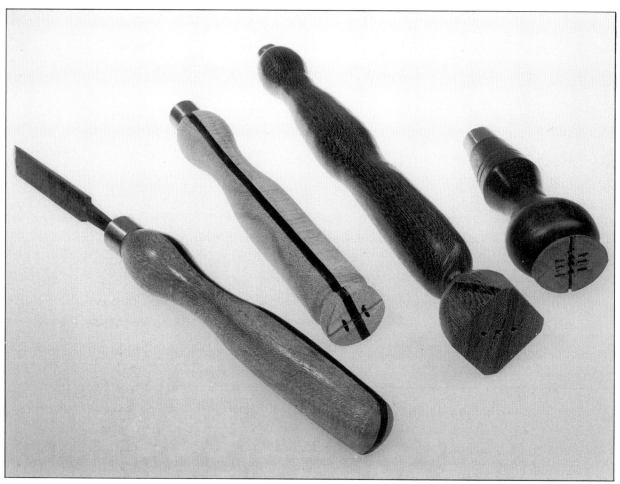

Fig 5.1 The leg.

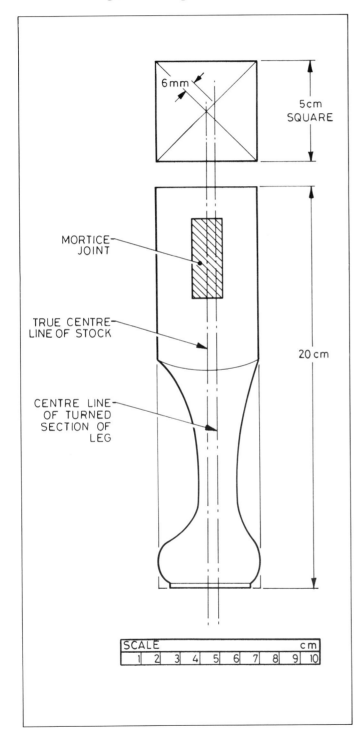

6mm

5cm
SQUARE

MORTICE
JOINT

TRUE CENTRE
LINE OF STOCK

CENTRE LINE
OF TURNED
SECTION OF
LEG

20 cm

SCALE   cm
1 | 2 | 3 | 4 | 5 | 6 | 7 | 8 | 9 | 10

Off-centre Foot

This method for turning a set of four legs with the feet off-centre would be the same whether you make them for a low stool or a full-size table. To turn the required profile, I suggest you first practise on an offcut about 20-30cm long.

The method shown is the one I would use to make a leg with the illusion of an off-centre foot; the dimensions, proportions and design should be whatever you decide will suit your piece of furniture.

I used 50mm square wood for this project – Fig 5.1 shows a finished leg with a mortice joint. If you are making a similar joint, remember to leave waste wood for a true centre to fit on your lathe. There is less danger of the finished work being damaged if the mortice is cut first.

Method

Mark the centres, one dead centre, the other 6mm away, at the foot on a diagonal line. Mark the centres with a pencil at both ends of the wood.

Fig 5.2 Turning a foot.

The off-centre mark will be the inside of the finished leg; the foot of each leg will then be facing outwards at 45° on the finished piece of furniture. Remember to put a saw cut across the centres to support the wings of the spur centre. The centres need only to be 6mm apart because, when the leg is turned, you actually remove 6mm from the back and leave 6mm on the front.

Now mount the workpiece between the true centres in its square section. Make sure the workpiece clears the toolrest before switching the lathe on, and then, gently but firmly, feed a roughing gouge towards the revolving wood and turn it down to a cylinder up to where it needs to be left square for the joint at the top of the leg. You can now start shaping the foot. At this stage, do not change to the off-centre mark, because it is not the foot that is off-centre: the leg is the section that needs to be turned on the off-centre mark.

The wood shown in Fig 5.2 shows a foot turned using the off-centre point on the left and a foot turned on the true centre point on the right – the one on the right is correct. When you move the work to the off-centre mark, revolve the work by hand to make sure it clears the toolrest before switching on the lathe. Complete the turning of the leg and foot, and finish with fine sandpaper.

Now comes the difficult part – making the other three legs to match the first one. You may find it helpful to make a template the same profile as the foot.

Fig 5.3 Finding the centres with a template.

Template for finding the centres

I have made a template for finding the centres: it is made from a piece of 9mm thick plywood cut to an L–shape, with a 45° set square screwed to it.

With this template you can find the centre of a square end of wood or a round piece of wood – a bowl blank, for instance – quickly and accurately. *See* Fig 5.3. If you do not have an old 45° set square handy, make your own from Perspex or Formica.

It can be seen from Fig 5.4 that the foot at the top makes the best use of the wood.

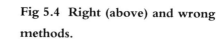

Fig 5.4 Right (above) and wrong methods.

CHAPTER 6

Egg Timer

T his project is turned between centres, using one true centre and one off-centre running parallel with the true centre. It is based on a standard glass, 76mm long x 14mm in diameter; three-minute egg timer glasses can be purchased from most craft supply outlets.

The project can also be scaled down to accommodate a spirit level bubble to make a pocket-sized spirit level, handy for touring, caravanners etc. If you make a spirit level, you will need to plane a few shavings off the back to stop it rolling about.

A piece of nicely marked wood 15cm long x 3cm in diameter is all that is needed: the timer case shown in Fig 6.1 was made from a small yew tree branch.

Method

Follow the sequence marked A, B, C, D and E in Fig 6.2.

A   Make saw cuts running parallel with each other at either end of the wood. Mark a true centre at each end and then an off-centre cut halfway between the true centre and the edge of the cylinder.

Fig 6.1 Egg timer turned from yew.

Fig 6.2 Method sequence.

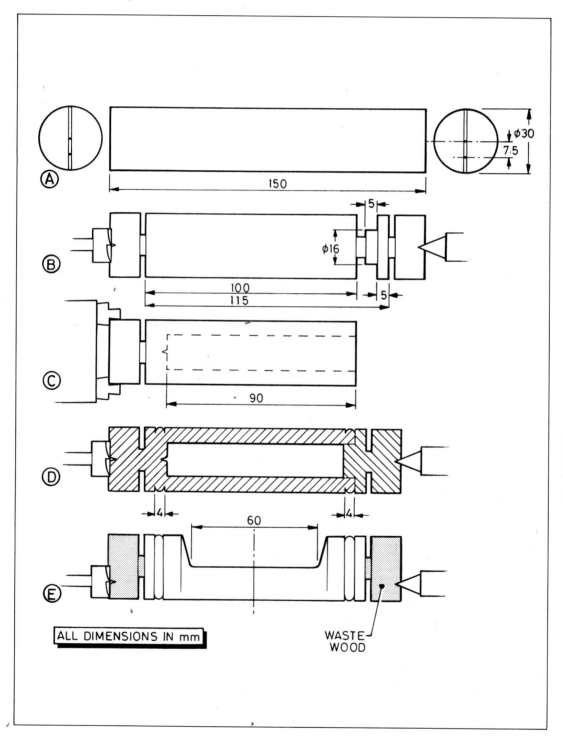

ALL DIMENSIONS IN mm

WASTE WOOD

B Make a cut for waste wood at each end with a parting tool, leaving 115mm in between for the project. You will be drilling a 16mm diameter hole to accept the glass timer; now is the time to make the stop end or bung for this hole. Turn the bung 16mm in diameter to be a snug fit for the hole.

C Fit the drive end of the project into a three-jaw chuck, a cupchuck or a spigot chuck, then drill a hole 9cm deep with a 16mm diameter sawtooth bit held in a chuck in the tailstock.

D Fit the stop end into the hole, and mount the work back between its true centres on the lathe. Turn a 4mm wide bead at each end; this will mask the stop end joint. Measure 3cm on both sides of the centre of the project and revolve the lathe by hand while holding a pencil on these marks.

E Remount the project on its two off-centre marks, revolve the lathe to ensure the toolrest is cleared, set the lathe speed at about 1100rpm and switch the lathe on. You will now see the pencil marks 6cm apart: this is for the window for the egg timer. You will also see a line where the wood looks solid and an area that appears blurred: it is this latter area between the pencil marks that is to be removed with a small spindle gouge (*see* Fig 6.3). Stop the lathe to check the work, then finish the cut with a small skew chisel. Clean off the sharp edges around the window with sandpaper, mount the project back on its true centres and finish with fine sandpaper and melamine

lacquer. When you remove the waste ends, make the cuts slightly concave so that the timer will stand firmly upright.

Remove the stop end; the glass tube can be held in place with a little ball of plasticine at each end. Replace the stop end and fix with a little glue. If you are making a spirit level, the glass tube can be held in with Polyfilla: set the glass tube in place with the Polyfilla, put the spirit level on a flat level surface and turn it end for end. When the bubble is in the middle, leave it until the Polyfilla has set.

Fig 6.3 Making the window.

Corkscrew Snake

I have turned a number of these snakes, and each one has been slightly different in shape – only to be expected from this particular species.

You may need to experiment first; once you have mastered the technique, almost any kind of hardwood will do: beech works well.

You may like to use a prominently-grained wood, Colombian pine for instance, as the result can produce unusual markings on the snake – *see* Fig 7.1.

The size of wood used obviously depends on the size of snake wanted: a good size to start with is about 30cm long x 5cm square. I made

Fig 7.1 A 'twist' of corkscrew snakes.

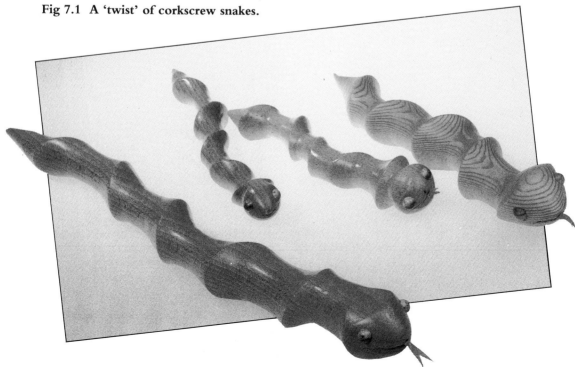

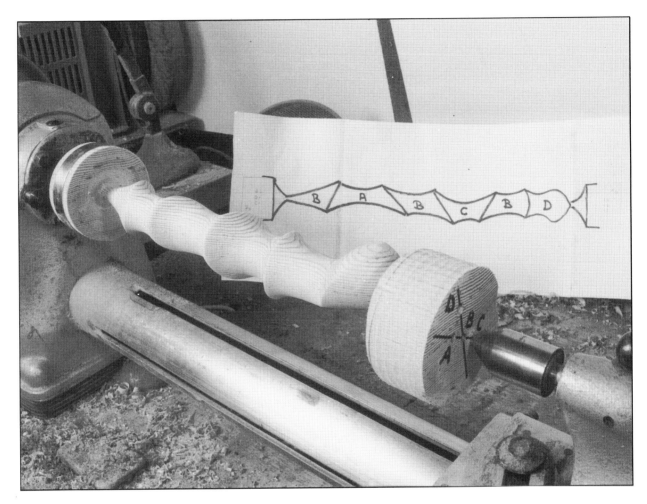

Fig 7.2 Setting out the proportions.

the cuts too close together on the first snake I produced with this method, and the finished article looked like a crankshaft out of a car engine. Study Fig 7.2 to get the right proportions.

Centres A, B and C run parallel with each other, B being the true centre. Off-centre mark D runs diagonally through the block; when the block is mounted on off-centre marks D, it is balanced. Centres D are only used to turn the shape of the head and to lift the head off the ground.

This project can be turned using only a sharp roughing gouge.

Method

Mark a centre line at each end of the block of wood. Cut along these lines with a saw to accommodate the drive spur wings. Mark true centres B and then mark off-centres A and C 9mm either side of B. Draw a line diagonally across the ends of the wood, and make a mark at D 15mm in from the centre mark, as shown in Figs 7.2 and 7.3.

Place the wood between the true centres B and turn it to a cylinder, leaving the two ends about 3cm long square as waste wood. Turn the sections marked B to a smaller diameter, making sure you do not reduce the tail section too much at this stage.

Remount the wood on to off-centres A and reduce the diameter marked A (*see* Fig 7.2), then remount to off-centre C and reduce the diameter marked C. At this point you will have reduced the diameter of five sections, only two of them off-centre.

Now mount the wood back on the true centres B and start to blend the angles in; do the same on off-centres A and C. Mount the work on off-centres D and begin to shape the head: if you have cut the shape correctly, the head will appear to be hooded. When satisfied with the shape, sandpaper and finish the head with melamine polish and wax. Remount the work on to centres A, and finish and polish as above, repeating the process with centres C.

Now remount the wood on to true centres B and finish the three sections marked B, and then part the waste blocks off at each end. To finish, turn two 5mm diameter pieces, domed at one end, for the eyes. Drill two 5mm diameter holes in the head for sockets, and glue

the eyes in. If you choose a wood for the eyes with different colours running through it, i.e. sapwood, the snake's eyes will appear half-closed.

Cut a slot for the mouth and glue in a forked tongue made from leather, plastic or a similar material. All that remains is to flatten the underside with a plane or belt sander, so that the snake will lie with its head off the ground and will not roll over.

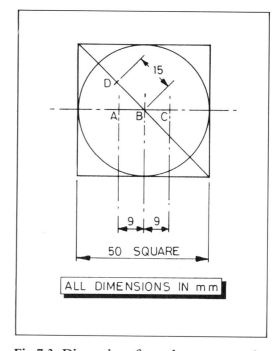

Fig 7.3 Dimensions from the centre mark.

Triangular Bud Vase

Fig 8.1 Marking out the true centres.

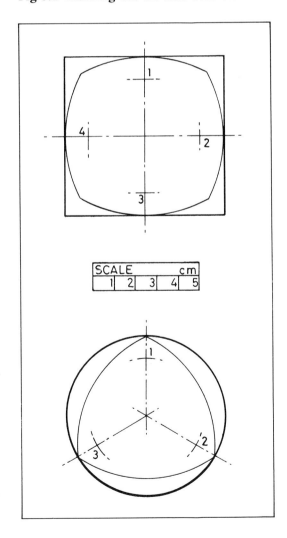

The wood for the bud vase needs to be 75mm square and about 180mm long. A 10cm x 15mm glass phial to hold water for the flower bud should be available at most craft supply outlets, although you can make your own from a suitable piece of plastic or metal tube; the bottom of the tube can be sealed with silicone mastic, which can be purchased in small tubes from an ironmonger. The following method could also be used on a dried grass vase; the wood would then have to be proportionally larger.

Method

First mark both ends of the wood with a true centre mark – Fig 8.1 illustrates setting out on the base of both a triangular vase and a square vase. For this project, mark the base with the three points shown in the illustration, and make a saw cut across these points to receive the wings of the drive spur. Now place the wood between centres on the lathe, using the true centres, and turn the whole length to a cylindrical shape with a roughing gouge, at a speed of about 1800rpm.

Cut away some of the wood to form a taper towards the tailstock from about halfway along the cylinder, as shown in Fig 8.2; this will help you to visualize the final shape of the vase when you multi-turn the lower part. Change the lathe speed to a slower speed, about 700rpm, and mount the wood on to one of the off-centre marks, having numbered the off-centre locations 1, 2 and 3; as you will be remounting the work a few times, this will help you select the correct centre for each cut.

Revolve the lathe by hand to ensure the work clears the toolrest before making a cut parallel with the toolrest, which should itself be parallel with the lathe bed. Repeat the cut on off-centres 2 and 3 and, if necessary, remount the work on any of the off-centre marks until

Fig 8.2 Forming a taper.

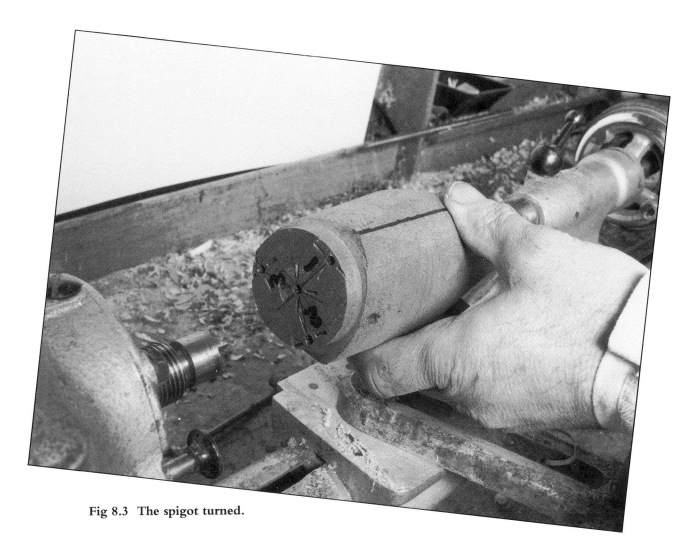

Fig 8.3 The spigot turned.

there is a triangular shape like that in Fig 8.1.

Using the toolrest as a guide, make three lines along the length of the wood at the corners of the triangle – *see* Fig 8.2. At this stage, you will need to go back to centres 1, 2 and 3 to make the final finishing cuts. First go back to off-centre 1, and remove some wood with a skew chisel until you have cut up to the lines; you may have to stop the lathe a few times to do this accurately. Rest the index finger of the hand supporting the tool blade against the toolrest, and try to make flowing

cuts – it may be helpful to use a scraper on the final cuts. The three faces can now be sandpapered while the lathe is stationary: wrap fine sandpaper round a block and hold it flat on the surface to prevent the corners of the triangular section becoming rounded over.

The vase needs to be mounted in a spigot chuck or a three-jaw chuck for drilling to receive the water holder. Place the vase in the lathe using the true centres, and turn the spigot – Fig 8.3 shows the vase at this stage. Remember that once you have turned the

Fig 8.4 Boring a hole for the water holder.

Fig 8.5 Finished vases.

spigot you will have lost the multi-centre locations, and you will not be able to do any more work on the triangular section.

Now mount the work in the spigot chuck or three-jaw chuck, and at a low speed bore a hole to receive the water holder, using a sawtooth bit mounted in a chuck in the tailstock – *see* Fig 8.4. This photograph also illustrates a multi-centre handle I made from mahogany for the tailstock; this gives me greater control and leverage when boring holes on the lathe in this manner.

Place a revolving centre in the tailstock and wind it into the water container hole, to provide support while you shape and finish the project. Once you have mastered the techniques and principle, you can experiment and perhaps add some decorative turning – Fig 8.5 shows two finished vases.

CHAPTER 9

Performing Seal

S eal is the general name given to a large group of sea mammals which are related to each other but are divided into three families: earless seals, eared seals (including sea lions) and walruses. The three groups are alike in many ways, so when turning this project you will not need to make a very precise shape or add a lot of detail. The finished piece leaves no doubt that it *is* a seal – of one kind or another (*see* Fig 9.1).

The important thing here is to get a good finish, with flowing lines; Fig 9.1 also shows that multi-centre turning alone is not going to

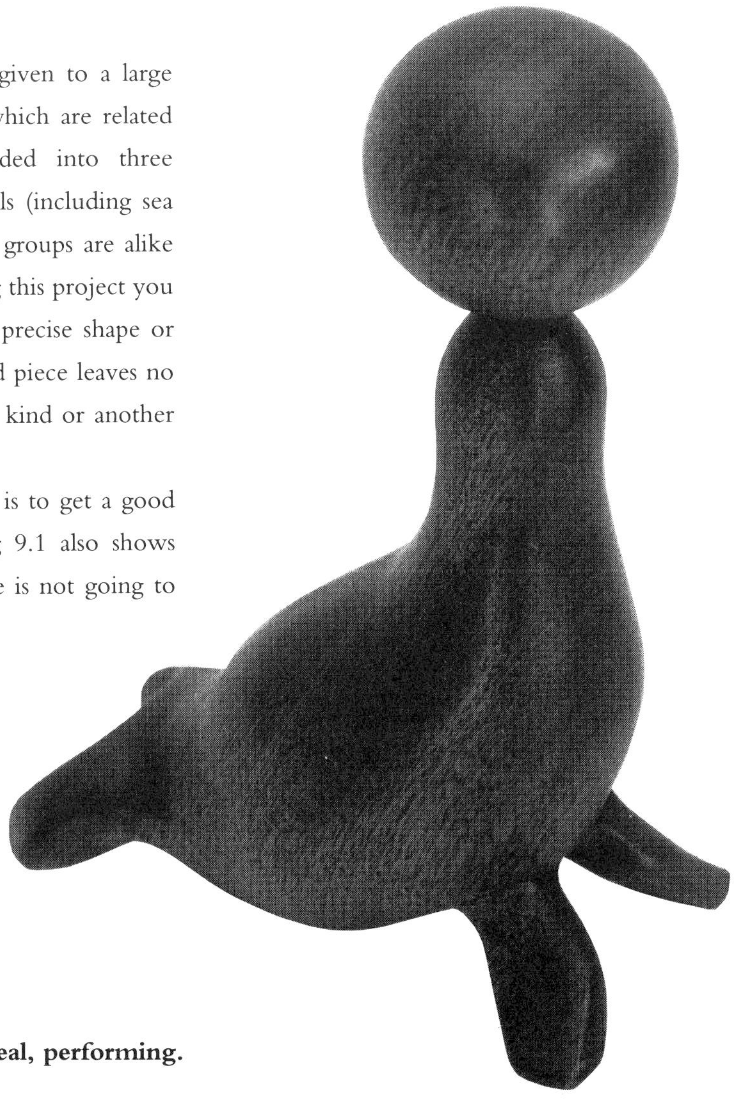

Fig 9.1 The seal, performing.

**Fig 9.2
Grain
direction.**

GRAIN DIRECTION

SCALE | | | | | | | | | cm
1 | 2 | 3 | 4 | 5 | 6 | 7 | 8 | 9 | 10

remove all the unwanted wood. After turning this project, I used the Arbotech woodcarver disc to remove most of the waste wood, and then finished with 2in (5cm) coarse and fine Velcro sandpaper discs. If you do not have access to an Arbotech disc, a wood rasp or Surform tool will suffice.

If you decide to use wood chisels or woodcarving tools, be careful where there are areas of short grain. To avoid some of this problem, the best way to set out the project is shown in Fig 9.2. The seal in the photographs was turned on a lathe with a 10cm swing; it is 18cm high and only just cleared the lathe bed.

I suggest you try this project on a piece of softwood first. You will need a piece of wood 6cm or 7cm thick, 15cm wide and 25cm long. Draw two lines on the wood, AA and BB, about 20° – 25° off the face edge, and begin to mark out the seal and ball. You may have to experiment a little when setting this out.

Method

Draw a rough outline of the seal and ball on the 25cm x 15cm face of the wood, bearing in mind that the two off-centre lines A-A and B-B, shown in Fig 9.3, should not be more than a 25° angle off the face edge, as the project would become too risky if the angle were greater. When satisfied with the drawing, it will be necessary to cut an area at right angles to each end of both off-centre lines. These areas have to be clear of the drawing of seal and ball and must be able to securely accept the drive spur at

one end and the tailstock at the other. You should now have an irregularly-shaped piece of wood, as seen in Fig 9.3.

Start to form the ball and the seal's head and neck on off-centre line A-A, using a small gouge with the cutting edge sharpened to a 'lady's fingernail'; then start to form the profile of the rear flippers and the body on line B-B, remembering not to remove any wood that will form the front flippers.

Go back to line A-A and finish the ball, head and neck; do not cut in too deeply between the ball and the seal's nose: it is not necessary, and you certainly won't want the ball to break off.

Finish the turned areas with sandpaper, and leave the project between centres on the lathe, locking or wedging the headstock shaft. This means the work is fixed firmly while you carve away the waste wood. Be careful when shaping the front flippers, as you will be working with short grain in this area.

Most of the wood can be removed with a coping saw; I found it very helpful to use a 2in (5cm) Velcro sanding disc in a pillar drill or bench drill. Use a coarse and then a fine sandpaper disc – hold the seal in both hands and move it around until you obtain flowing lines. It is important to wear a dustmask for this operation.

Finish by hand with fine sandpaper, and apply a coat of melamine lacquer; when dry, rub all over with 0000 steel wool and apply a second coat of melamine.

**Fig 9.3
Off-centre
lines.**

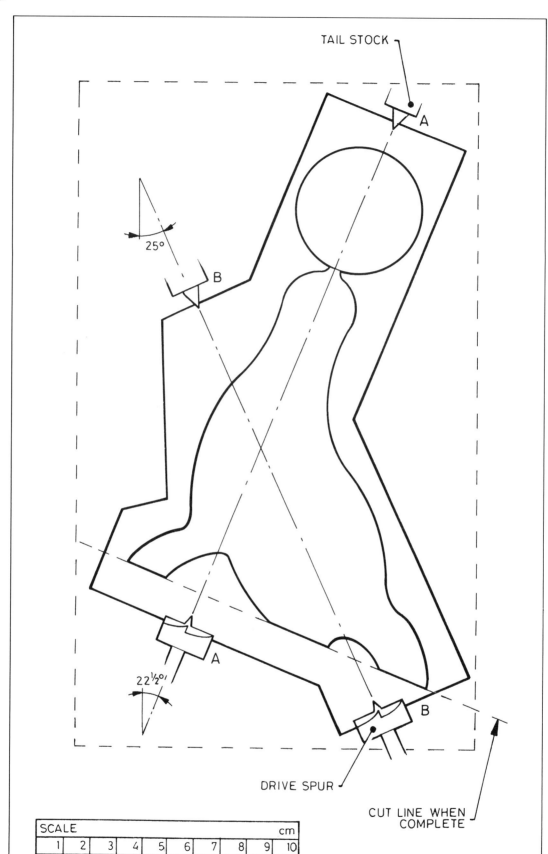

TAIL STOCK

A

25°

B

22½°

A

DRIVE SPUR

B

CUT LINE WHEN
COMPLETE

SCALE									cm
1	2	3	4	5	6	7	8	9	10

Walking Sticks

The aim of this project is to make a natural stick with a turned handle in one piece. The material needs to be a fairly straight stick up to about 92cm (3ft) long and 5-10cm in diameter. Most types of wood can be used, but it is better to select a type you can identify –

Fig 10.1 Two centres for the handle.

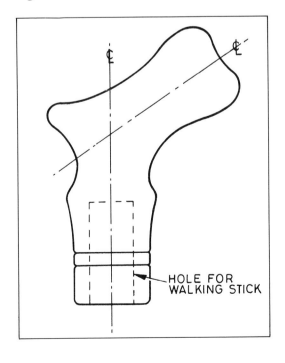

yew, ash, oak, maple or whatever. When the outer bark is peeled off cherrywood, the underbark resembles leather: this makes an interesting combination with the wood on a finished stick.

When selecting your material, try to find a stick that can be cut with a section of adjoining branch left on, so it can be turned as a handle, or select a piece of branch separately and turn the handle on its own before fitting it to the stick. The handle in Fig 10.1 was turned using two centres, and was made from a branch of wood already curved at an angle.

The finished sticks look very attractive and sell well at craft shows; they have a little label attached, saying, 'A walking stick is not only for the infirm, it is a constant companion with no backchat.' Steel end caps can be purchased at most craft supply centres.

Jig

You will really need a three- or four-jaw chuck with independently adjustable jaws for this exercise; if this is not available to you, there is

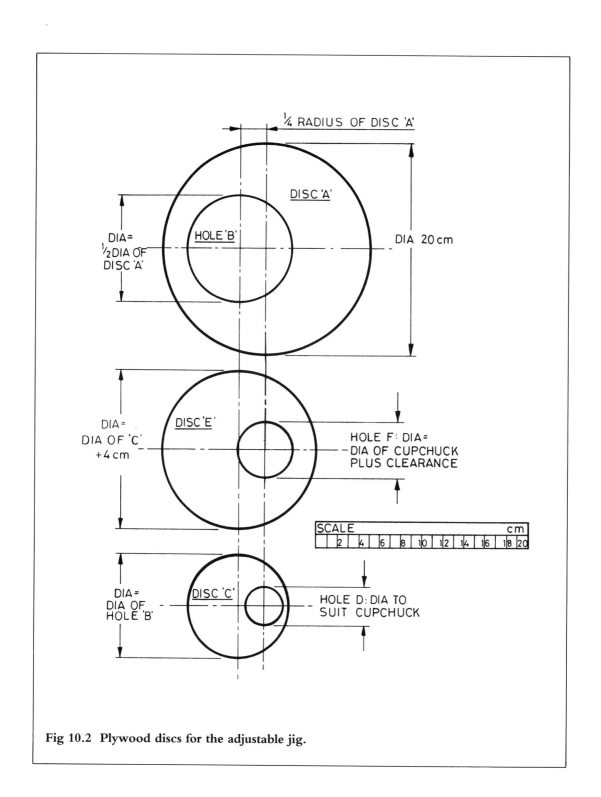

¼ RADIUS OF DISC 'A'

DISC 'A'

HOLE 'B'

DIA=
½ DIA OF
DISC 'A'

DIA 20 cm

DISC 'E'

DIA =
DIA OF 'C'
+4 cm

HOLE F: DIA=
DIA OF CUPCHUCK
PLUS CLEARANCE

SCALE   cm
| 2 | 4 | 6 | 8 | 10 | 12 | 14 | 16 | 18 | 20 |

DISC 'C'

DIA=
DIA OF
HOLE 'B'

HOLE D: DIA TO
SUIT CUPCHUCK

Fig 10.2 Plywood discs for the adjustable jig.

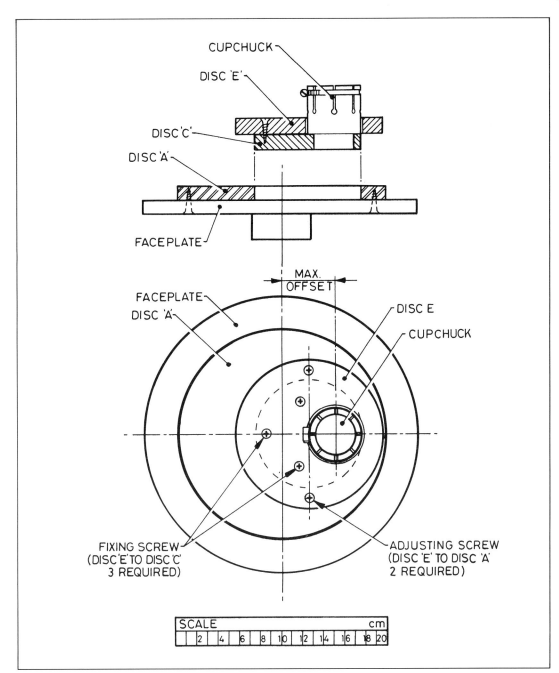

Fig 10.3
Fitting the
cupchuck.

another way. One jig I have designed for multi-centre turning is particularly useful for this project. **This jig must only be used at low speeds**. An adjustable cupchuck is secured to the jig – this cupchuck is fully described in Chapter 12.

To understand the formula for this jig, it is important to first study Fig 10.2. The adjustment range on the jig is true centre to

5cm off-centre. The plywood discs and the off-centre holes can all be cut on a faceplate; before screwing the plywood on to the faceplate, place some scrap hardboard between the disc and the faceplate to avoid damaging the faceplate.

The largest plywood disc for this jig is 20cm in diameter, but whatever size jig you make, the formula will be the same (*see* Fig 10.2): mark a 20cm diameter circle on a piece

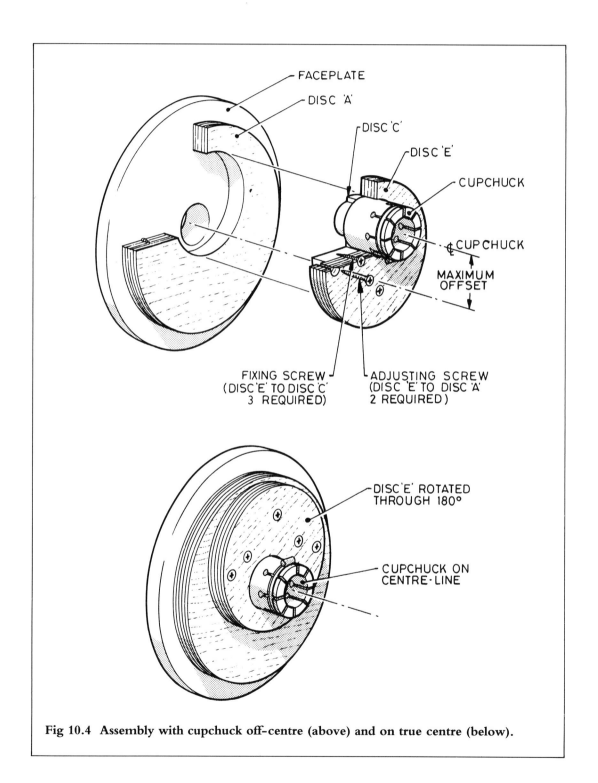

Fig 10.4 Assembly with cupchuck off-centre (above) and on true centre (below).

Fig 10.5
Using a
revolving
cupchuck to
turn the
stick end.

of 18mm thick plywood (disc A). Half the radius of this disc will be the centre of the second disc (disc C), which will be 10cm in diameter.

Half the radius of disc C will be the centre point for the cupchuck (hole D); this centre point should now be lined up with the centre of disc A, and a 10cm diameter hole (hole B) can now be cut in disc A.

The cupchuck should now be fitted and glued to disc C – *see* Fig 10.3. To hold the jig together, cut a 12mm thick plywood disc (disc E) with a diameter 4cm more than the diameter of disc C. The centre of the hole in disc E is half the radius of disc C, and the diameter of the hole is large enough to fit over the cupchuck. (Fig 10.4 shows that if disc E is revolved half a circle, the centre will be the true centre.)

The outside diameter of the cupchuck for this project is 5cm, and the inside diameter is 3.5cm. Disc E should be permanently screwed to disc C. The cupchuck can be positioned anywhere between true centre and maximum off-centre, and then secured; the complete assembly, with the cupchuck at maximum adjustment, is shown in Fig 10.4.

The 2cm overlap of disc E is for the screws securing it to disc A; two screws opposite each other should be sufficient. If the jig is used a lot and the adjusting screws in disc A become elongated, they can be re-sited around disc E or it might be easier to replace disc A.

Method

Fit the stick between centres on the lathe, first brushing off any dust or mud with a wire brush. It is advisable to wear a pair of protective gloves for this project, as well as the usual face shield.

Fig 10.7 Removing wood along a mark.

Switch on the lathe at its slowest speed – this may look a bit disconcerting, but if you feel the stick is not too bent for this project, carry on.

Now turn down the end of the stick at the tailstock end to a diameter to fit the steel end cap. If you have a revolving cupchuck, that will be ideal for this project – *see* Fig 10.5.

The next step is to partly turn what will be the handle. Allow about 3cm at the end of the stick, and turn to 3.5cm diameter – this is to fit in the three- or four-jaw chuck or the adjustable cupchuck. The idea behind partly

Fig 10.6 Head turned off-centre.

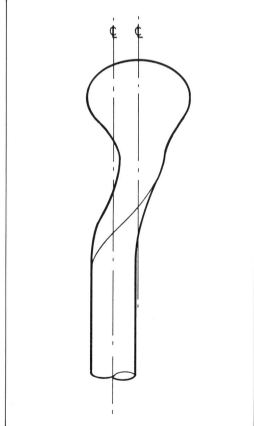

turning the handle is to get rid of some of the waste wood and to help you visualize the finished shape.

Now carefully feed a bowl gouge or roughing gouge to any part of the stick that is not running too far off-centre. Any part of the stick cut by the bowl gouge will now need to be finished with a skew chisel and sandpaper. Shift centre at the drive end of the lathe, and repeat the operation, feeding in the turning tools gently. While the head of the stick is off-centre, turn the handle: some interesting blends of angles will begin to appear (*see* Fig 10.6).

The tendency when turning sticks is to make them a bit heavy. Don't be afraid to remove the wood – you are making a stick, not a weapon! If the stick does not look balanced or is too heavy in places when you have finished turning, remove some more wood while the stick is held between centres, using an Arbotec woodcarving disc. It will help to mark the area

to be removed with a black felt-tip pen – *see* Fig 10.7. You can use a spokeshave, a plane or a Surform tool as substitutes for the Arbotec. Try keeping the area you remove by hand flat, as this will produce more angles and make the stick more interesting.

Fig 10.8 shows a stick at the finishing stage – the finish on most of my woodturning is wax, oil or melamine, but I make an exception with sticks, preferring to use varnish. I believe this finish will stand up to the weather and that it enhances certain characteristics in the sticks.

No two sticks will be the same, as you can see from the selection in Fig 10.9; the sticks lying in front of the rack show the wood selected for multi-turning, and the stick shown in the photographs for this chapter is resting against the rack.

Fig 10.8 Varnishing a stick.

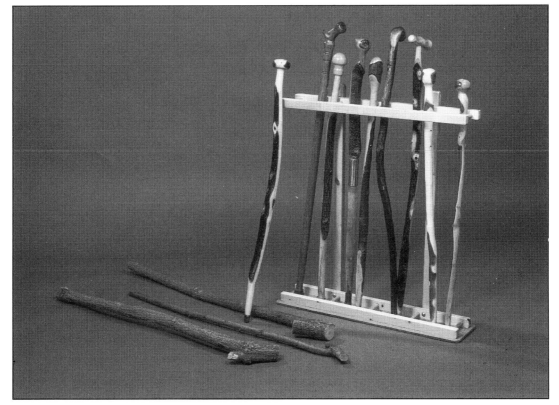

Fig 10.9 A selection of walking sticks.

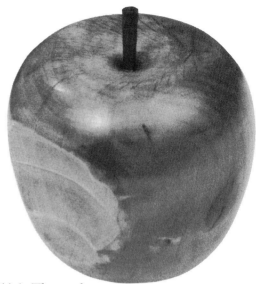

Fig 11.1 The apple.

CHAPTER 1 1

Apple

I n this project we are going to take a bite out of the forbidden fruit!

When we buy fruit and vegetables, they are not always nice and round and symmetrical: sometimes there are defects and bad patches, or the fruit is misshapen. This can be simulated with multi-centre turning: we can select wood with defects that can be reflected in the fruit. For instance, if the wood has splits in it, the apple is a windfall; a spalted piece of wood or one with wormholes in it can equally look authentic.

The fruits and vegetables in this and the following chapters will be dyed with food colouring, which is ideal for such projects. I use red, blue, green and yellow; these colours can be blended to produce new colours, and they can be diluted with water. This is a big advantage over spirit stains, as any colour you get on your hands or in places it is not wanted can easily be removed with water.

When selecting the wooden blocks for the fruits and vegetables, you will need light-coloured wood to take the food colouring. Sycamore, lime, hornbeam, holly or wood from fruit trees – apple, pear or plum – are all suitable.

First we will make an apple with a bite taken out of it; in fact there will be two apples, because the wooden block for this project has to be mounted off-centre in a simple jig on a faceplate. Two blocks 8cm x 8cm x 11cm long are needed to balance the work.

Jig

The jig is simple to construct: a 25cm diameter disc is cut from 12mm thick plywood and is then screwed to a faceplate. Two strips of 2cm square wood are screwed to the plywood disc to securely accept the 8cm square blocks, as illustrated in Fig 11.2.

Method

Before using the jig, place the blocks between centres and slightly undercut the wood at the drive end of the lathe with a parting tool. Take the corners off along the length of the block and turn a large radius at the tailstock end leaving a small section for remounting the block between centres (*see* Fig 11.3).

Fix the two blocks securely to the jig with screws, then place one end of the toolrest between the blocks and rotate the blocks – if they clear the toolrest, secure the toolrest

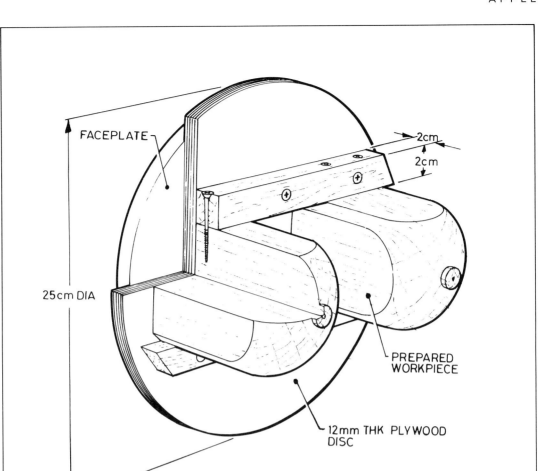

FACEPLATE

2cm

2cm

25cm DIA

PREPARED
WORKPIECE

12mm THK PLYWOOD
DISC

Fig 11.2 Making the jig.

Fig 11.3 Wooden block ready for mounting in the jig.

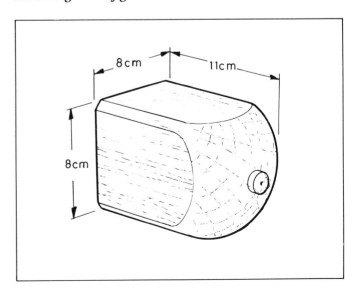

8cm

11cm

8cm

firmly. When the lathe is switched on at a slow speed, it should run smoothly if the jig and material have been fixed correctly.

The bite

The bite should be made first. Mark the bite position with a black marker pen; when the lathe is switched on, these marks will be visible. To form the bite, use a scraper shaped like (and called) a lady's fingernail, with a half-round profile: gently feed the tool in, as if turning the inside of an egg cup or goblet, making the bite deep enough for turning the apple. Make about four grooves, stopping the lathe a few times to check the shape of the bite. There is no need to form a perfect bite, as not many people have a perfect set of teeth. This operation can be seen in Fig 11.4. I have demonstrated this dozens of times and have never once had my knuckles rapped or had a mishap, but it should still be performed with great care.

Remove the blocks from the jig and place one of the blocks between centres; the drive spur should be driven into the centre of the waste end of the block. Run the lathe at a faster speed, and start to form the shape of an apple with a roughing gouge. Reduce the waste end to a diameter that will fit a spigot chuck; place the partly formed block in the spigot chuck, and finish shaping the apple, taking care not to reduce the bite too much. Finish with 400 grit sandpaper.

Fig 11.4 Forming the bite.

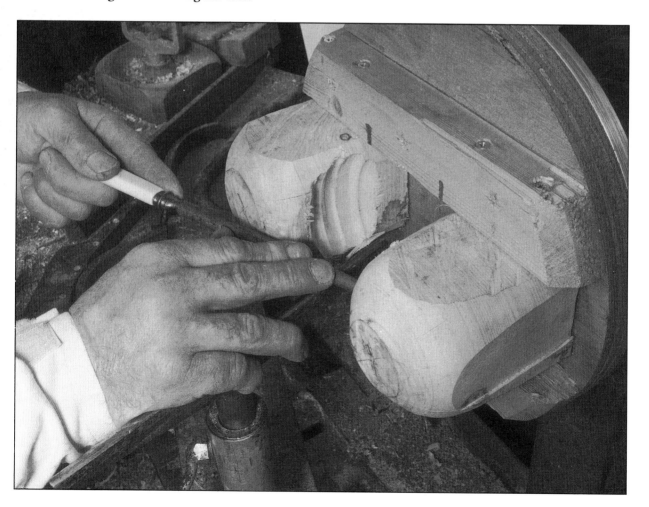

Fig 11.5 Drilling a hole for the stalk.

Drill a 3mm hole in the top of the apple for the stalk – this can be drilled with a hand-held drill while the work is revolving (*see* Fig 11.5); the stalk can be turned later.

The blip

Part the apple off the waste wood to about 5mm with a parting tool. Twist the apple off: this will leave a 'blip' similar to that on a real apple - *see* Fig 11.6. Colour this blip with a black felt-tipped pen; an alternative is to drill a hole in the bottom of the apple and fit and glue a clove into the hole. This can also look very authentic.

The stalk

The stalk can be turned carefully between centres, supporting the work and a small skew chisel between finger and thumb. You might prefer to cut a suitable twig, from a bush or

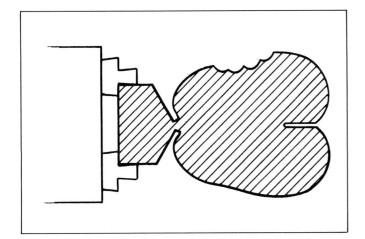

Fig 11.6 Making the blip.

Fig 11.7 Hanging up to dry.

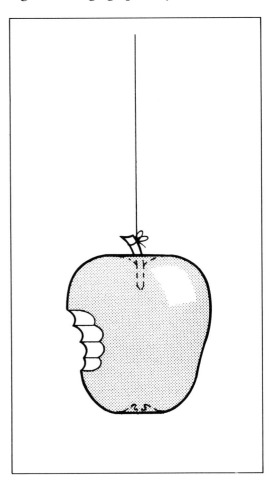

hedge, to give an authentic touch. To assemble, simply glue the stalk into the previously drilled hole.

Polishing

Apply two coats of melamine polish over the bite, to prevent the coloured dye from staining it; when this is dry, dilute some green food dye with water and apply it all over the apple with a soft brush or a piece of cloth. While this is still wet, apply some diluted red colouring to one side of the apple, and blend in with the green. When the dye is dry, glue the stalk in the previously drilled hole; allow it to dry, and then apply two coats of melamine polish all over the apple with a soft brush. Suspend the apple by its stalk from a length of cotton thread, and allow to dry (*see* Fig 11.7).

Follow this procedure with the other block, and you will have two apples; they probably won't be exactly the same, but what two apples are?

Avocado in Two Halves

T his project involves faceplate turning and turning between centres. The avocado needs to be held in a cupchuck: *see* below for how to make a simple adjustable cupchuck.

The material for the avocado should be close-grained, light-coloured wood - lime would be the best choice, with sycamore and holly close behind. You will need two pieces 20cm long and 6cm wide; one should be 30mm thick, and the other 45mm thick.

Fig 12.1. Avocado.

Fig 12.2 Cupchucks - one with a spigot.

I used a spindle gouge to form the avocado shape; a skew chisel would normally be used to remove the tooling marks, but this will not be necessary here, as we want to simulate the texture of an avocado skin. This way you are also spared the skew chisel's nasty habit of digging in at a crucial point.

Adjustable Cupchuck

This is an alternative to a rigid cupchuck: the material can be the same size, and there is not much more work involved. Fig 12.2 shows two cupchucks: one will fit in a three- or four-jawed scroll chuck, and the other has a spigot turned on it, to fit in a spigot chuck.

The wood should be a hardwood, preferably with a bit of spring: ash, yew,

Fig 12.3

Half sphere and flat surface.

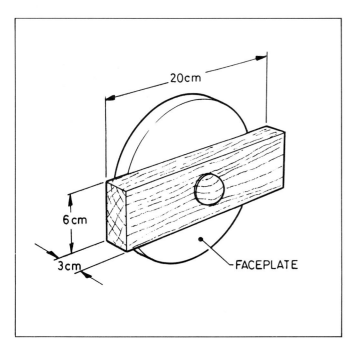

hickory or similar. When setting up to make this cupchuck, you might like to make two or three different sizes: I have made one for holding eggs to finish off the ends, which works very well.

This chuck is adjustable up to 5mm in diameter. *See* below for making a rigid cupchuck. When this has been made, turn a 1mm deep recess near the top of the cup to accept a Jubilee clip. Drill eight equally spaced 5mm holes around the bottom of the cup, and make a saw cut down to each hole from the top. This cupchuck is also used in Chapter 10. When using it, remember to keep your hands clear of the Jubilee clip.

Method

Fix the 45mm thick piece of wood across the centre of the faceplate using woodscrews. Turn a half sphere in the centre of it to 30mm diameter, 15mm radius; this will leave a thickness of 30mm on the rest of the workpiece. This surface must now be turned flat – *see* Fig 12.3.

Now carefully reduce the sphere at its widest diameter by about 1mm, which in effect gives you slightly more than half a sphere projecting above the flat surface, and will help you get a snug fit for the next part of the project. Take the 30mm piece of wood and fit it across the faceplate in the same way, this time turning an inverted half sphere. Fig 12.4 shows both sections.

Turn the second half to be a push fit on

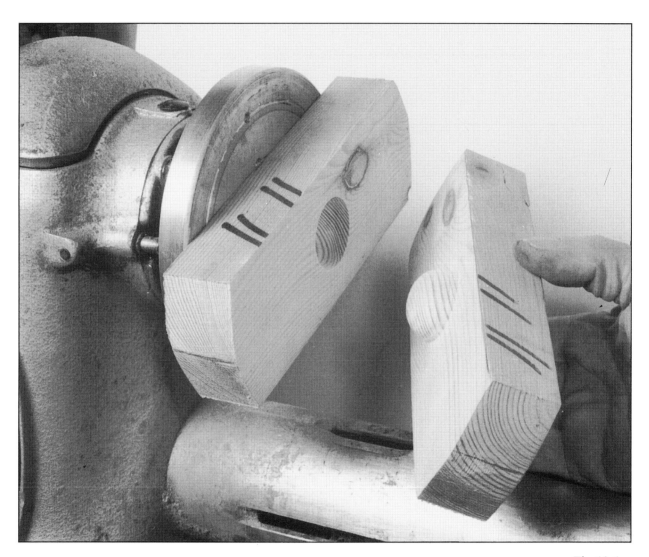

Fig 12.4
Both half
sections.

the previously turned half. Screw the two pieces together and mount them between centres, as shown in Fig 12.5. Turn the shape of an avocado, leaving enough wood at each end to hold the project between centres for the next stage, simulating the texture of the skin.

This is achieved by using a spur-type grinding wheel dresser. The round washers should be removed first, and the star-shaped wheels left in. By pressing this tool on the revolving work at a slow speed, you can get the required texture, but the first time I attempted the project, this almost disappeared when I applied the water-based dyes. This is because when a little water is applied to areas of wood that have been compressed, the water swells the

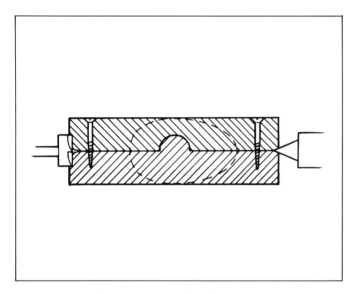

Fig 12.5 Mounting between centres.

grain where there are small dents, and when dry the wood becomes almost flat again.

To get and keep the right texture, the method is to apply the dents with the grinding wheel dresser as shown above, and when the wood is dry, to sandpaper it more or less smooth. Wrap the avocado in a wet tissue, thus wetting the wood; as it dries, the texture should appear. This may take more than one attempt, depending on the kind of wood you use some woods will provide a better texture than others.

If you do not have a grinding wheel dresser, there is an alternative method: grind or file the point off a 7cm or 10cm nail, and polish it with sandpaper or emery cloth to form a half ball section. Gently tap the ball section all over the avocado with a hammer, and sandpaper the wood smooth. When the wood is wetted, the texture should appear as described above.

Rigid Cupchuck

Carefully part the waste off each end of the avocado. To finish the ends, you may make a rigid cupchuck for the project. Turn a piece of wood about 12cm long x about 10cm square to a cylinder, then turn one end to fit a spigot chuck. After securing this cylinder in the spigot chuck, form a cup in the free end with a gouge or small bowl gouge. Make this cup section just big enough to fit the avocado, placing a piece of cloth or tissue in the cup to prevent damage to the avocado's surface. Finish turning the ends and complete the textured finish as above.

To colour the outside of the avocado, experiment with a blend of green, yellow and blue food dyes; a diluted yellow on the inside surfaces will complete the colouring. The stone or seed can be left its natural colour. Finish by sealing both halves with cellulose sealer or melamine polish; the completed project can be seen in the colour section.

CHAPTER 1 3

Pear, Aubergine and Banana

Thesе projects are grouped together because they are turned using the same method. There will be no new jigs to make as they are all turned between centres.

Pear

A piece of sycamore or holly will be ideal; a piece 10cm square and 25cm long will be ideal for a full-sized pear. Fig 13.2 shows the setting out on both ends of the block. The diagonal lines at each end of the block run parallel to one another. The letter M on the true centre marks stands for 'middle'. When the block is mounted between centres on the M centre, it is to turn the diameter of the pear's middle section. If you were to turn the rest of the pear

Fig 13.1 Banana and aubergine.

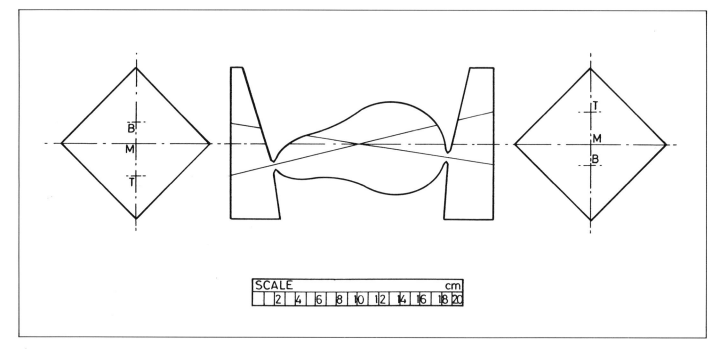

Fig 13.2

Setting out

the pear.

on these true centres, the result would be a perfectly symmetrical pear – not the object of the exercise.

The two off-centre locations marked T are the centres for turning the top of the pear: they are marked 3cm off-centre, while the two off-centre locations marked B are for mounting the block to turn the bottom section. The B marks are only 2cm off-centre to make the most use of the wood; this means that a larger radius for the bottom of the pear can be achieved.

Fig 13.3 shows the nearly finished pear mounted between centres on the lathe. It is mounted on its true centres, i.e. when the two cuts seen in the photo were made. The angles on the waste pieces were made when the block

was mounted on its off-centre locations. Mark the ends of the block as shown in Fig 13.2, and make saw cuts along the diagonal lines to receive the wings of the drive spur.

Method

Set the lathe speed at around 1100rpm, and mount the block between its true centres. Turn the wood to a cylinder with a roughing gouge, leaving about 35mm each end square; if you cut too much off the ends, you will lose the off-centre locations. Continue turning the middle section of the block to about 6cm, making sure you do not remove too much wood at the tailstock end, as this will be the bottom end of the pear.

The block is now ready to be mounted off-centre. Set the lathe at a slow speed, around 700rpm, and mount the work between centres on the B marks, making sure the drive centre has entered the saw cut. Revolve the lathe by hand to check that the block clears the toolrest, then start the lathe. It can be a bit off-putting to see the block revolving on the off-centre marks, but remember that one end of the pear is off-centre one way as much as the other end is off-centre the other way, so the block is perfectly balanced. If you get vibrations, there is something wrong.

Gently feed in a roughing gouge and roughly shape the bottom end of the pear. Remove the block from the lathe, remount it on the off-centres T and start to shape the top. Do not remove too much wood at the extreme

Fig 13.3 Pear mounted between centres.

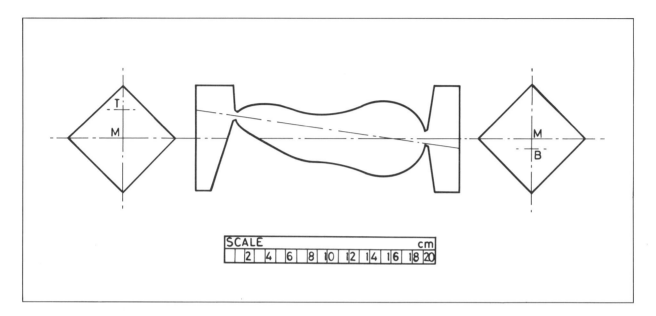

**Fig 13.4
Setting
out the
aubergine.**

ends of the pear shape at this stage, as the waste ends could easily break off. Now gently shape the pear and blend the angles in with sandpaper.

It is important to mark the centres with letters: when I was experimenting with making the first multi-centre pear, I found it easy to get the centres mixed up. The result was that the first pear was quite straight, but the blip on the bottom was off-centre.

Remove the waste blocks from each end, and finish the pear in exactly the same way as described for the apple in Chapter 11, even down to blending a little red dye: this is a contrast to the green, and will make it look more attractive. The finished pear can be seen in the chestnut burr bowl in the colour section.

Aubergine

Before starting this project, it is recommended that you study the shape and texture of a real aubergine: note the bell shape of the stalk and cap. The project uses the same working method as for the pear, but has only two centres – *see* Fig 13.4.

The wood block can be the same size as that of the pear, but need not be a light colour: a piece of mahogany is quite suitable, as the finished article is dark and can be made to look authentic by mixing a little neat blue and red food dyes together. The ideal size of wood is 25cm long and 7- 8cm square.

Method

The setting out in Fig 13.4 shows the marks for

Fig 13.5 Aubergine mounted between centres.

the top and bottom ends; the middle line is just to help blend the angles. The centre marks for the lines T and B need to be marked as far away from the true centre mark as practicable to get a secure fixing for the centre spur and the tailstock centre. After this line has passed through the waste wood sections, it will then be right for achieving maximum curve on the aubergine. Make a saw cut for the drive spur wings, mount the block between true centres and turn the whole length to a cylinder at a lathe speed of 1100rpm. Remove some wood from the centre, then mount on mark B and shape the bottom. Change to mark T and shape the top. Fig 13.5

shows the aubergine taking shape.

At this stage, only a gouge or skew chisel have been used; coarse and fine sandpaper are all that will be needed to finish.

Refer to Fig 13.6 to make the stalk and bell shape for the top: turn a light-coloured piece of wood to fit over the top of the completed aubergine. When this bell is parted off, there will probably be a small blip left inside; remove enough wood from the top of the aubergine to accommodate the blip, and the bell should then fit snugly. Dye it neat green and glue it on. The completed aubergine can be seen in the colour section.

**Fig 13.6
Aubergine
stalk and
bell.**

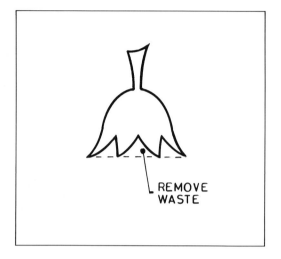

Banana

This project has three centres, and is turned in the same way as the pear and aubergine, although it is more difficult than the latter. Some of the waste wood should be cut away on a bandsaw or by hand with a coping saw – *see* Fig 13.7.

The wood should be 10cm x 4cm x 25cm long. The piece of wood used here was the white sapwood of the yew tree: neat yellow food dye gives an authentic touch. When I cut this piece off the plank, I left some of the brown wood on it, and the brown patch was still there when the banana was finished - well, that's true to life: if I am offered bananas, I usually pick the overripe one.

Given the suggested size of the wood, you might think it would be better, and just as quick, to cut two or three bananas from it on a bandsaw and shape them by hand with a spokeshave. But that is not what this book is about: it is about showing methods for jig and chucking systems for multi-centre turning, and for you to develop you own ideas, observing safe working practice and having the satisfaction of producing an article in a way that possibly nobody else has attempted.

Fig 13.7 Setting out the banana.

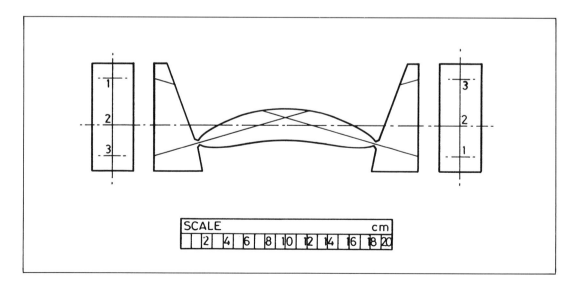

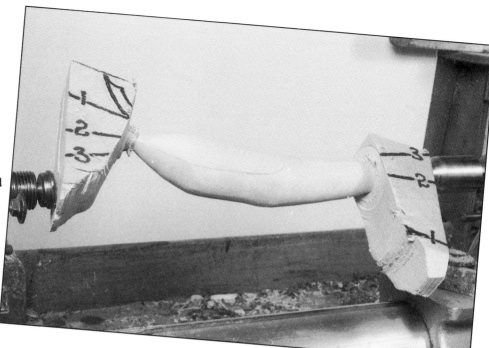

**Fig 13.8
Banana mounted
between centres.**

Method

Draw a line down the centre of the wood, then take a real banana and place it on the wood and draw two more lines, following the contours of the fruit as in Fig 13.7. This illustration and Fig 13.8 both show that the minimum amount of waste wood has been left; this must not, however, be too small, or there is a risk of pressure from the tailstock fracturing the workpiece at the short grain area.

Mark a line 1cm around the banana shape on the wood, mark the waste wood and square the lines down the sides (*see* Fig 13.7). Make a 5mm deep saw cut for the drive spur wings and mark for mounting between centres. Cut the waste wood away and put it in your box of useful pieces for small turning projects.

Mark the ends of the lines 1, 2 and 3 as shown in Fig 13.7. Set the lathe to 1100rpm and turn some wood off centre line 2. Change centres to line 3, remove more wood, and then repeat the procedure for line 1. As a guide, place the real banana in a convenient place in

front of you. Don't eat it yet – you will find that difficult anyway, as you should be wearing your face shield.

Turn off more wood, remounting on lines 1, 2 and 3 as necessary; Fig 13.8 shows the shape forming between centres. When you have a banana shape, wrap a piece of medium sandpaper round a flat block of wood and rub some flats on the banana. Be careful not to remove too much wood: if you study your real banana, the flats are not very prominent.

When satisfied with the shape, colour the banana with neat yellow dye, apply a little green dye at both ends and darken the tips with a black felt-tip pen. An alternative method of achieving an authentic finish is to use a pyrograph tool for the markings: spots and lines can be burned in, and brown patches can be made by slowly sweeping the hot wire over a small area. If you carefully shape the waste wood at one end, this will produce a stalk, which can also be darkened. Fig 13.1 shows a stalk darkened with a pyrograph tool.

CHAPTER 14

Peppers

Before attempting to turn a pepper, it is worth studying some: they are not very symmetrical and vary in shape, but this is not a problem, as it can be simulated in multi-centre turning by the use of a simple jig.

You will also notice that the colouring varies, from dark green to yellow, orange and bright red, or a combination as one side ripens before the other. Food colours do not seem to fade – even the reds hold their colour well – so use a piece of light-coloured wood, 15cm long x 10cm square, to make the best use of the colours.

Preliminary Turning

Place the block between centres and turn to a cylindrical shape. True up both ends with the parting tool, slightly undercutting the face supported by the tailstock, and cut a radius on the end supported by the headstock. The concave undercut is made so that the block will sit firmly on the plywood faceplate jig; the radius will be at the top of the pepper.

Jig

The jig is made up of three discs of 12mm plywood (*see* Fig 14.1). Cut one disc the same size as your faceplate: this will be disc A. The faceplate used in this project is 30cm in diameter, but a smaller size would work. Cut a disc 16cm in diameter – this will be disc B – and cut a disc 20cm in diameter (disc C). A 12cm diameter hole should be cut out of disc C.

All these cuts can be made on the lathe by first fixing each of the discs on the faceplate, having placed a piece of hardboard on to the faceplate to avoid damaging it when cutting out the disc with a parting tool. When cutting discs for jigs on a faceplate, it is not necessary to use high speeds: these are usually associated with getting a fine finish. I also prefer to use lower speeds for this procedure as the plywood corners fly off with less force.

Fix disc A 35mm off-centre to the faceplate. Start the lathe, cut a 16cm diameter hole with the parting tool and mark a 20cm diameter circle around this hole with a pencil. Disc B should fit neatly into the hole, and the pencil line will also help you centralize disc C.

Method

Now screw disc A centrally on to the faceplate. Take the wooden block and place the concave end in the centre of disc B, fixing it firmly with three or four screws. Place disc B and the block into the hole in disc A on the faceplate, and place disc C centrally over the top, lining it up with the pencil mark made earlier. Use four screws to fix disc C to disc A – Fig 14.2 shows a plan of the jig with the block attached.

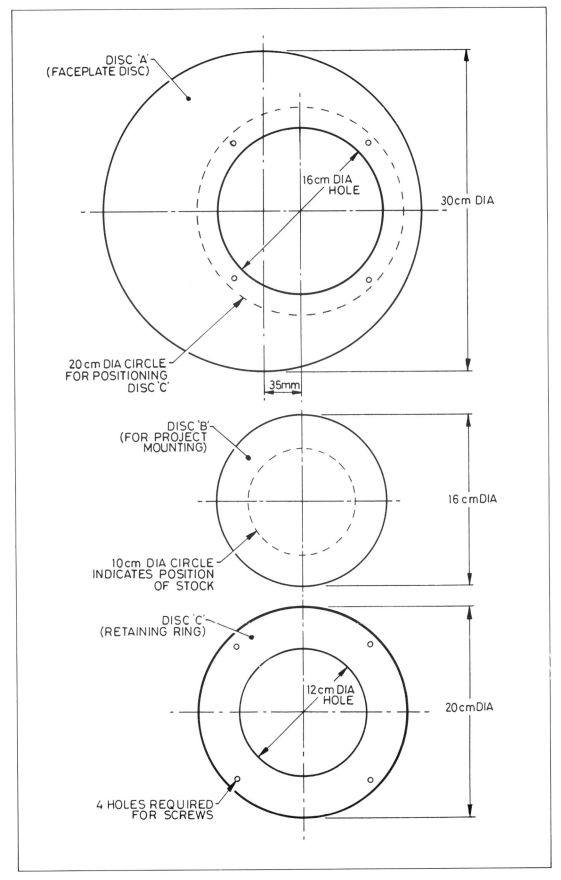

DISC 'A'
(FACEPLATE DISC)

16 cm DIA
HOLE

30 cm DIA

20 cm DIA CIRCLE
FOR POSITIONING
DISC 'C'

35 mm

DISC 'B'
(FOR PROJECT
MOUNTING)

16 cm DIA

10 cm DIA CIRCLE
INDICATES POSITION
OF STOCK

DISC 'C'
(RETAINING RING)

12 cm DIA
HOLE

20 cm DIA

4 HOLES REQUIRED
FOR SCREWS

Fig 14.1
Discs for
the jig.

Fig 14.2
Jig with the
block
attached.

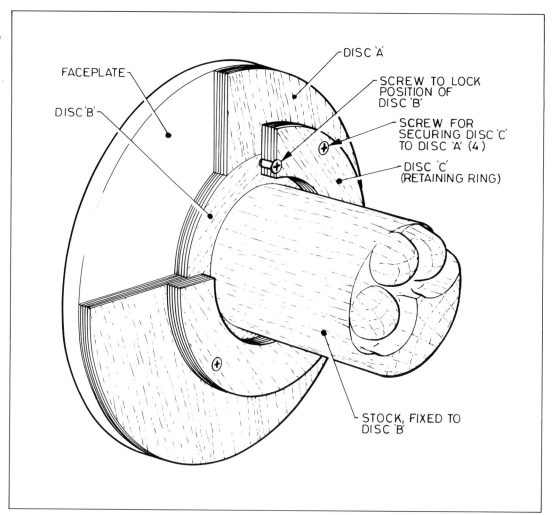

FACEPLATE

DISC 'B'

DISC 'A'

SCREW TO LOCK
POSITION OF
DISC 'B'

SCREW FOR
SECURING DISC 'C'
TO DISC 'A' (4)

DISC 'C'
(RETAINING RING)

STOCK, FIXED TO
DISC 'B'

The block of wood is now trapped off-centre on the faceplate; it does not need to be counterbalanced, as it is only 35mm off-centre. If the screws holding down disc C are loosened slightly, the block can be revolved and repositioned; one screw through disc C into disc B will lock the block in the selected position. Tighten all the screws, stand clear and start the lathe at about 1100rpm.

While the lathe is running, carefully make a mark or small circle on the end of the wooden block with a pencil resting on the toolrest, in line with the new centre; this will be the position of the first dome. Form this dome with a small gouge, and square a pencil line from the centre of the dome down the block on to disc C. This mark will be the datum - the point for marking the positions of

Fig 14.3
Turning the domes.

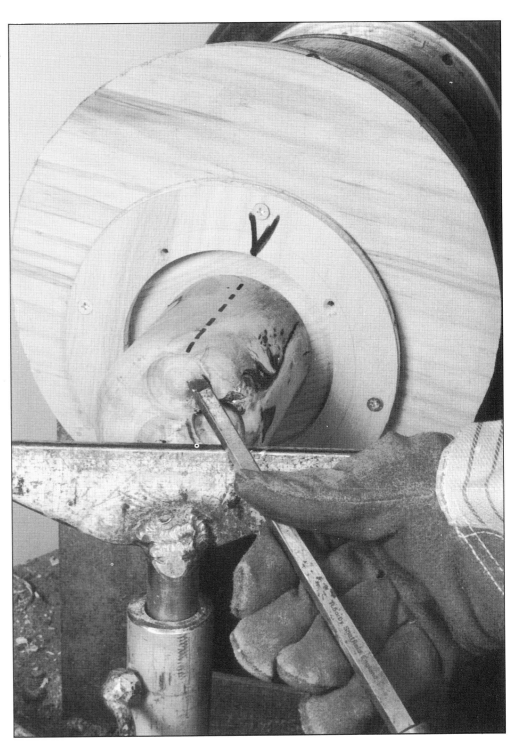

the remaining domes (*see* Fig 14.3).

Decide where you are going to position the next dome, and square a pencil line down the block, remove the single screw, line up the pencil line with the datum mark, replace the screw and secure the new position, and form the next dome. After turning a couple of domes, you will find it unnecessary to square a line down to the datum mark, as this can be judged by eye. As you finish turning each dome, carefully give it a complete finish with fine sandpaper; by rolling or folding the sandpaper and applying it to the domes, you can keep your fingers clear of the revolving work. This operation can be seen in Fig 14.3.

The domes do not have to be the same diameter, or even the same height. On some peppers they are in pairs. Place them where you like; whatever you decide will be right: even a defect in the wood can influence you. As long as the completed pepper has a good finish to it, it will be suitable; after all, we did not set out to make perfect symmetrical specimens – life is not like that. If you are a multi-centre turner, you have what is known as artistic license!

When the domes are completed, remove the block from the faceplate jig and fit it to turn between centres on the lathe. In the length of wood for this project, I allowed for a spigot to be turned for an adjustable cupchuck, a spigot chuck or a three-jaw chuck. Turn a spigot at what will be the bottom of the pepper, place the block in the chuck and drill a 20mm hole about 25mm deep in the top of the pepper, for use later. The tailstock centre can be wound into this hole to support the block while the rest of the work is being done.

If your lathe does not have the facility to lock the headstock pulley, secure the work with a wedge to stop it rotating. The pepper will need some hand work to finish the shape; this involves cutting waste wood from between the domes with a wood chisel and then cutting small valleys down part of the length of the pepper. Finish shaping with coarse sandpaper or a flapwheel, and then with fine sandpaper and a Velcro disc in an electric drill.

Fig 14.4 Turning the stalk.

Fig 14.5 Finishing the stalk.

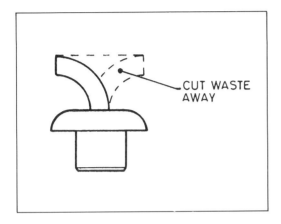

The stalk should be made from 10cm x 50mm square light-coloured wood. Turn a cylinder to fit a 4cm spigot chuck, turning the end bell-shaped to form the curved stalk, as shown in Fig 14.4. Turn part of the spigot end to 20mm diameter to fit in the pepper. Cut most of the bell-shaped end away with a small saw, leaving enough wood to form a curved stalk; this can be shaped with a file and sandpaper (*see* Fig 14.5).

Dye the stalk with neat green food colouring before fixing and gluing it into the hole at the top. The pepper can be dyed with neat red dye on one side and, while still wet, a blend of orange and red on the other, or green - whatever you feel will be appropriate. When the dye has dried, brush on two coats of melamine polish and hang the finished pepper up to dry.

The pepper in Fig 14.6 was turned from a block of diseased *catoni aster* wood: after making the domes on the faceplate jig, I mounted the block between centres and turned it to a cylindrical shape. To remove most of the diseased section, I mounted the bottom end of the pepper off-centre; this gave the pepper a tired, sagging look. It is a long time since it occupied a position in the front row of the greengrocers' shop window – in fact, it looks like its days are numbered.

This is the last multi-centre fruit project – by using the methods described and adding a little imagination, it is possible to make a variety of other fruits and vegetables.

Fig 14.6 The 'tired, sagging' pepper.

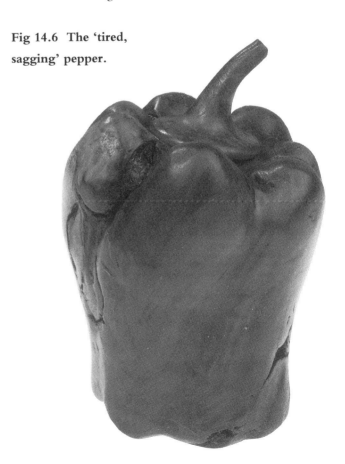

Pen Set Holder

T his was my first multi-centre project: I thought it would be nice to have a black and red trumpet-type pen set holder, so I turned two pointed domes, fitted the pens to the domes and mounted the domes on a piece of figured elm. When I presented the set to my wife, the comment was that it looked like the profile of a lady's chest. Well! You can imagine how I felt; I went straight back to the drawing board and designed my first multi-centre turning project. This project won an award and was featured in *Winning Designs for Woodturning* (Unwin Hyman).

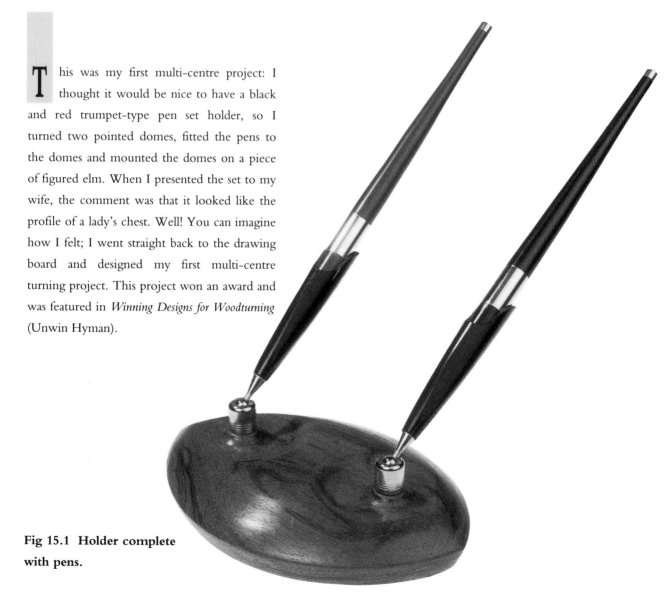

Fig 15.1 Holder complete with pens.

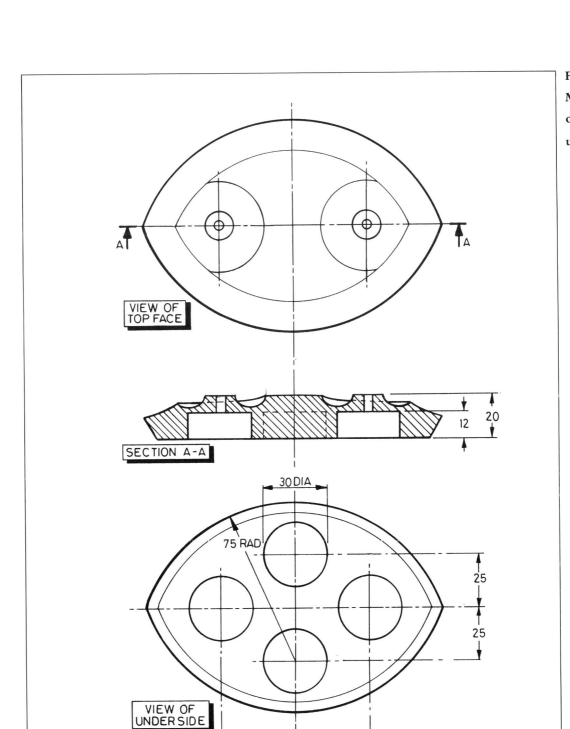

Fig 15.2
Marking
out the
underside.

VIEW OF
TOP FACE

SECTION A-A

20

12

VIEW OF
UNDERSIDE

30 DIA

75 RAD

25

25

35

35

Method

Select a well-marked piece of hardwood, 15cm x 10cm x 25mm; the trumpet pens can be purchased from craft supply outlets. First look at the finished item in Fig 15.1. It is important to accurately set out the block of wood: mark two centre lines at right angles to each other, and mark two points 35mm each side of the centre across the length and 25mm each side of the centre across the width (*see* Fig 15.2).

Using a compass, strike an arc from each of the 25mm points to meet the centre line at the ends of the block. Cut round the arcs with a bandsaw - *see* Fig 15.3. Make a 3cm diameter hole 12mm deep on each of the four points marked on the block, using a sawtooth bit.

Fig 15.3 The arcs cut and ready for mounting.

Fig 15.4 Shaping the top face.

Turn the petal shape of the wood: select one of the holes 25mm off-centre and place it over the jaws of a three-jaw scroll chuck, opening the jaws with a chuck key so they expand in the hole. If necessary, gently tap the wood home with a mallet to make sure it is seated squarely on the jaws. Give the chuck key another small turn to ensure the work is secure, but do not overdo it, as the jaws will split the wood if they are opened too far. Make sure the toolrest is clear, and start the lathe at a slow speed, gently feed in a gouge or scraper to make a clean profile, and shape the top face (*see* Fig 15.4).

Move the chuck to the opposite hole and finish the profile and the shaping of the top;

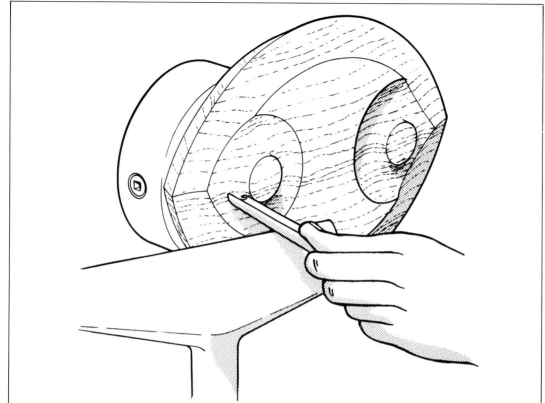

Fig 15.5 Blending in a dished section.

Fig 15.6 Finishing with a sandpaper block.

now move the chuck to the remaining holes and form the plinth for the trumpet pens, and blend a dished section into the top of the wood (*see* Fig 15.5). It will only take a few seconds to remove and remount the wood on the chuck for cleaning up and polishing.

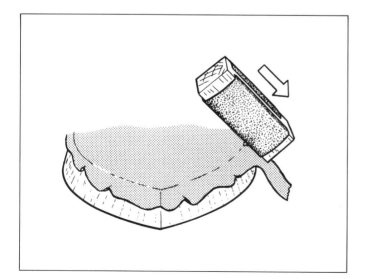

Jig

This project can be turned on a faceplate if you do not have the appropriate chuck: cut a 12mm thick plywood disc 20cm in diameter, and screw it to the faceplate. Glue a 9mm thick disc 3cm in diameter to the centre; the holes in the block can then be placed over the small disc and secured to the large disc with screws. The method is then the same as on the three-jaw chuck.

Holders

When the project has been finished, drill two small holes through the plinth and fit the trumpet pen holders. To complete the project, glue a piece of green felt or baize to the underside. This can be trimmed to size and finished to have a clean edge by wrapping a piece of sandpaper round a block and rubbing the felt towards the edge as shown in Fig 15.6.

Banana, avocado and aubergine.

Decorative bowls.

Pepper.

Fantasy bowls.

Ring stand.

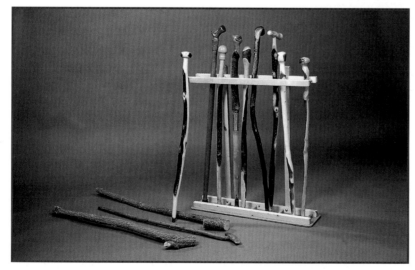

Walking sticks.

Platter on signboard.

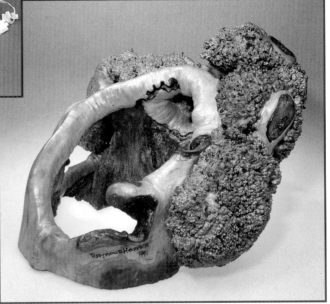

Burr.

Burr flower in vase.

Vases.

Corkscrew snakes.

Chestnut burr bowls.

Decorated orbs.

Oval tool handles.

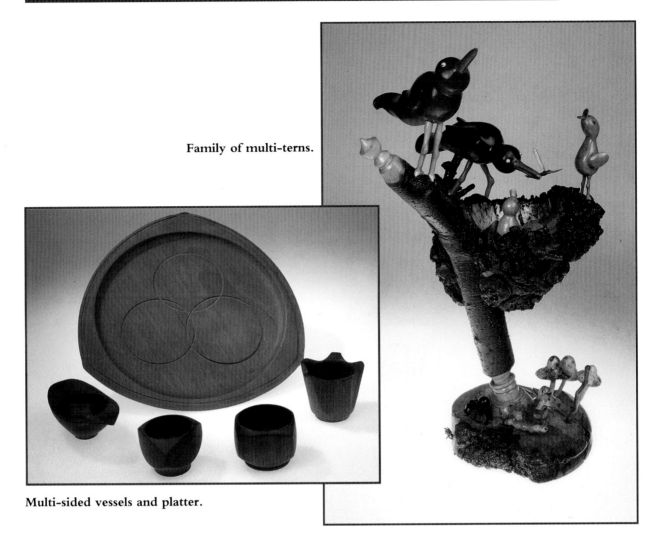

Family of multi-terns.

Multi-sided vessels and platter.

Caddy spoons.

Egg timer.

Decorative platters.

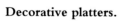

Decorative platters.

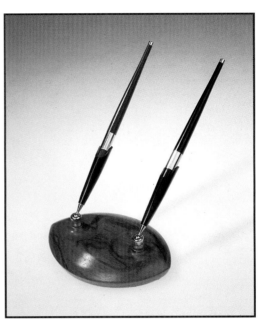

Pen set holder.

Snow scene.

Triangular bud vases.

Jarrah burr bowl
and turned fruit.

Wine coasters.

Spheres.

Apple.

Ring Stand

T o make this project, you will first have to construct a simple jig with an adjustable counterbalance. This jig is also useful for similar projects; it is designed for a 15cm diameter faceplate – *see* Fig 16.2.

Jig

Cut plywood discs 15cm in diameter, and build them up to a thickness of approximately 5cm; any thickness of plywood will do, and it is a good way of using up offcuts. When assembling the discs, one can be cut in half and a gap can be left for the counterbalance bolt or studding. Glue and screw the discs together.

Screw the jig to the faceplate and turn a chamfer on it as shown in Fig 16.2; this chamfer is to allow room for a screwdriver when attaching or removing workpieces. Fix a 9mm plywood disc to the plywood, using only screws as it may need to be changed for a

Fig 16.1

The ring stand in use.

Fig 16.2
The jig.

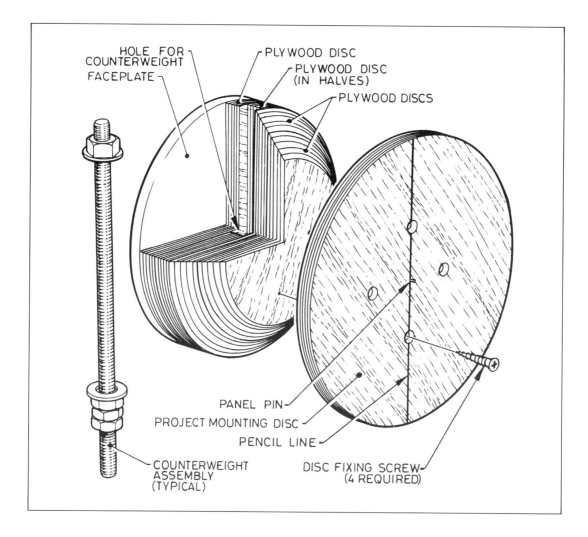

HOLE FOR
COUNTERWEIGHT
FACEPLATE

PLYWOOD DISC

PLYWOOD DISC
(IN HALVES)

PLYWOOD DISCS

PANEL PIN
PROJECT MOUNTING DISC
PENCIL LINE

COUNTERWEIGHT
ASSEMBLY
(TYPICAL)

DISC FIXING SCREW
(4 REQUIRED)

different sized disc. This top disc is for mounting the projects on, and can be increased in diameter if necessary. But do not be too ambitious, as great care is needed when using a counterbalance jig: make sure the fixings are secure, and keep clear of the revolving parts. It is very important that you wear a face shield and gloves for this project. The balance of this jig can be adjusted by the number of nuts on the bolt, or by the distance they are from the end.

Assemble the jig on the faceplate without the bolt, mount it on the lathe and clean and true it up. Make a pencil line across the centre of the face of the jig, parallel with the counterweight bolt; this is for correctly lining up the workpiece. Make a mark in the centre and drive in a panel pin, leaving the head projecting about 2mm; this will be used to correctly position the project.

Method

The completed ring stand is shown in Fig 16.1. You will need two pieces of hardwood: one should be cut to an 18cm diameter disc 25mm thick, and the other should be 12cm x 25mm square, for the ring post.

Divide the circumference of the disc into three equal sections. Make a dead centre mark on the underside and draw a line from this mark to each of the three circumference marks; square these lines round on to the face side of the disc. Make a mark halfway along these lines

and drill a hole at each mark. The holes should just be big enough to fit neatly over the projecting panel pin on the jig face (*see* Fig 16.3). These three holes will be the true centres of the three dishes.

Place one of the holes in the disc over the panel pin in the jig. Line one of the three points on the circumference with the pencil line on the jig and fix with screws through the plywood. Position the screws to be between the dished recesses on the finished work – *see* Fig 16.3.

It is now important to balance the project: with the jig and workpiece mounted on the lathe, remove the drive belt so that the jig can

Fig 16.3 Marking out the plywood disc.

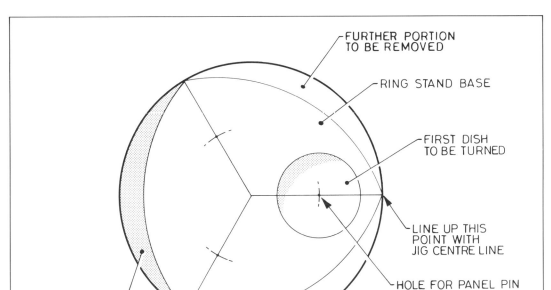

**Fig 16.4
The dishes
turned out.**

turn freely. Remove or add nuts along the counterweight bolt, or screw them along the bolt until the jig is balanced. Now start the lathe at a slow speed; if the balance is correct, there should be no vibration and the lathe should run as smoothly as if there were no work mounted on it. There will probably be some air disturbance, which will remind you to keep clear of the revolving parts.

Draw a line on the overhanging section of the disc by resting a pencil on the toolrest and revolving the jig by hand; the line should meet the edge of the disc at points marked earlier on the edge, so the line will equal $\frac{1}{3}$ of the circumference. Draw over this line with a black felt-tipped pen. Revolve the jig and mark the section in the true centre for the dish size, again with a black felt-tip. With the lathe running at

a slow speed, cut through the overhanging section of the disc on the pen mark, using a parting tool.

Shape this raw edge with a gouge and finish with sandpaper. Now turn the dish out with a small gouge, first making sure that the screws holding the disc to the jig will be clear of this recess. Repeat the procedure for the remaining two sections. The recesses need not match each other, and the dish section can have vertical sides or be rounded over, as shown in Fig 16.1.

Drill a 9mm hole in the centre of the disc, and then turn the ring stem, which is held between centres with a 9mm spigot. Glue the stem into the hole in the disc and finish with melamine polish.

Wine Coasters

Fig 17.1 A set of coasters.

This project, like the ring stand, uses a true centre, to first turn the wood cylindrical, and three off-centre locations. This time, however, we will make some decoration on the face, where the tailstock would normally be positioned.

The material should be hardwood or a close-grained wood: I used purpleheart, but this can be quite unkind, especially when turning

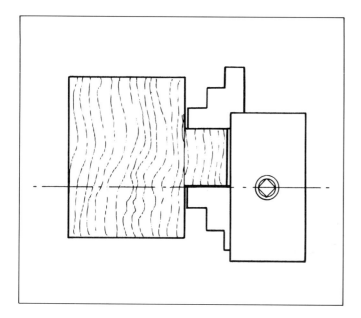

Fig 17.2 Setting the chuck jaws out of position.

Fig 17.3 Marking the face.

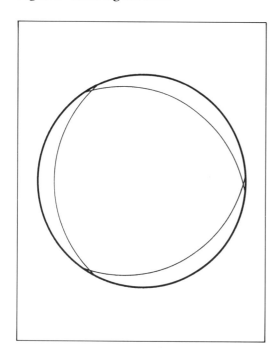

the diameter against the grain. Unless you are very careful, bits can fly off. Easier woods to turn for this project are Brazilian mahogany, beech or similar; whatever wood you choose, the tools will need to be kept very sharp.

A set of six coasters can be made from a 10cm cube of wood – *see* Fig 17.1.

Method

Mark two true centres on the block to turn it cylindrical. The centres are not marked in the conventional way, on the end grain: they have to be marked on two opposing long grain faces for this project. You will need to put a saw cut on the drive side for the spur, as you will be cutting the end grain; this can put a strain on the mounting of this size block. The block must be cut circular, preferably with a bandsaw, before fitting on the lathe.

Mount the wood on the lathe, making sure the spur wings enter the saw cut, and turn to a cylindrical shape. Turn a spigot to fit in a scroll chuck at the drive end of the block. One of the jaws of the chuck needs to be placed out of position: it must project outwards so that the block is about 18mm off-centre when placed in the chuck – *see* Fig 17.2.

The size of the chuck will determine the diameter of the spigot: a large diameter spigot will give the block better support. If your chuck has reversible jaws, that will be better still; a four-jaw chuck can be used in the same way for this project. If you do not possess a three- or four-jaw scroll chuck, the adjustable cupchuck described in Chapter 10 can be used for this project.

Place the block in the chuck that is now set about 18mm off-centre, and tighten the jaws enough to dent the spigot; you will use these dents quite a few times to accurately remount the block. Number the indents 1, 2 and 3. If you use the adjustable cupchuck jig, these positions can be marked on the project

and the cupchuck with a shallow saw cut. With the block mounted in the chuck at 1, revolve the lathe by hand and mark a line on the face of the block about $\frac{1}{3}$ of the circumference, using a pencil resting on the toolrest. Remount the block to positions 2 and 3, repeating the marking; there may be some trial and error here to begin with, but the result should be as seen in Fig 17.3.

Fig 17.4 Fitting the cap over the point.

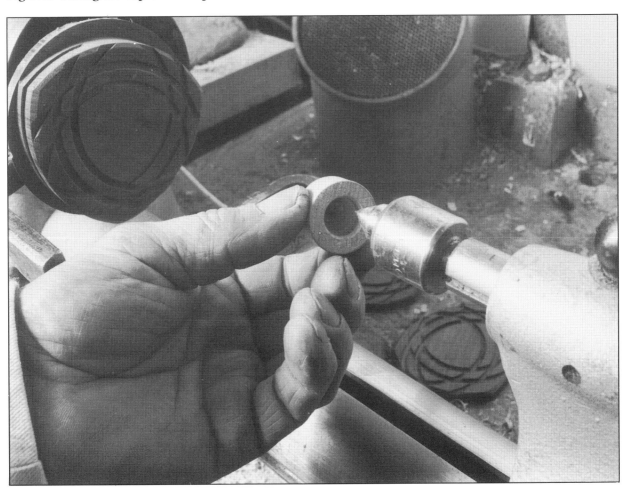

**Fig 17.5
The cap
supports
the block.**

The area outside the triangular shape is waste wood, which must be gently removed with the scraper at a slow lathe speed, about 700rpm; the block will need to be mounted in all three positions for this. If you possess a revolving centre, turn a wooden cap to fit over the point (*see* Fig 17.4), then move the tailstock towards the block so that the cap is pressed against the block to support it – *see* Fig 17.5. When this is complete, you will have a triangular-shaped block mounted off-centre in the chuck, ready to have the coaster design marked on it.

The design should be cut with a parting tool with a blade about 3mm wide; the tool must be kept sharp all the time to get clean cuts. First mark the design on the face of the block with a pencil, using the same method as when marking out the triangular shape; the finished design on the face will look like that in Fig 17.6. Before making a cut, go over the pencil mark with a black marker pen: when the lathe is switched on, you will be able to see this line, which indicates the position of the first cut. Gently feed in the parting tool and make a cut 2mm deep.

Stop the lathe, mark along the pencil line parallel with the first cut with the marker pen, and turn it out as before (*see* Fig 17.7). Now make a 2mm chamfer on the outer edge. Repeat this procedure on the block in its other two positions. The design is now complete on the first coaster, and you can clean up the face with fine sandpaper before

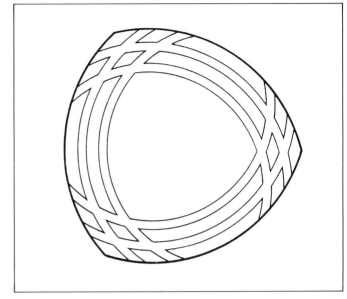

Fig 17.6 Finished design on the face.

cutting the coaster off the block with a parting tool – the coaster should be 6mm thick.

You will be cutting the coaster off a block that is revolving round off-centre. Wind the tailstock up to give the block support, and feed the parting tool in very gently; for the cleanest cut, set the lathe speed at about 1100rpm. Do not make the cut right through: it is better to stop the lathe and finish off the parting with a hacksaw.

Once you have made one of these coasters, you will find the rest of the set comparatively easy to produce. As each one is parted off, clean up the face of the block and check it is flat; I use the back edge of an old hacksaw blade for this. To finish, rub with fine sandpaper and apply two coats of melamine or Danish oil with a fine brush.

**Fig 17.7
Turning
out the
design.**

Decorative Platters

Whatever area of woodturning is attempted, there are always new geometrical or artistic designs or shapes to create. The attractiveness of the platters in this project depends on the geometric designs you can achieve; the finished platters are shown in the colour section.

Jig 1

Two plywood jigs were developed for this project: the first was designed for a 15cm diameter faceplate, and is 18mm thick. (See below for the second jig.) With this jig set up as in Fig 18.1, the platter can be turned in four positions 5cm off-centre. The 9cm square of plywood will be held in position with a hex-headed bolt and wingnut through the faceplate. Note the weights that keep the faceplate balanced (*see* below for details): a 6mm thick plywood disc is mounted on the 9cm square of plywood to locate the platter blank. The diameter of this disc should correspond with the diameter of the recess in the back of the project, made for the spigot chuck. In this

project I used a 45mm diameter spigot chuck.

Method

The platter blank is 25mm thick x 20cm in diameter, with a recess turned into it to fit a spigot chuck, and a recess cut in the base with a parting tool to correspond with the holding screws in the 9cm square jig (*see* Fig 18.2). Shape the back, seal with sander sealer and finish with wax or melamine polish. Mount the blank on the spigot chuck and face off the top of the platter.

The platter is now ready to be mounted on to the jig; it is held by short screws which go through holes in the 9cm square plywood (*see* Fig 18.1) into the platter. The screw holes will not be obvious if they are located in the recess – *see* Fig 18.2. This 'jig on a jig' can now be mounted with the hex-headed bolt and wingnut.

Jig for felt-tip pen

Three grooves 1cm apart will need to be made in each of the four positions with a parting tool, and I have made a jig for a felt-tip pen. There is a small panel pin in this jig, which can be

Fig 18.1

Jig 1 set up.

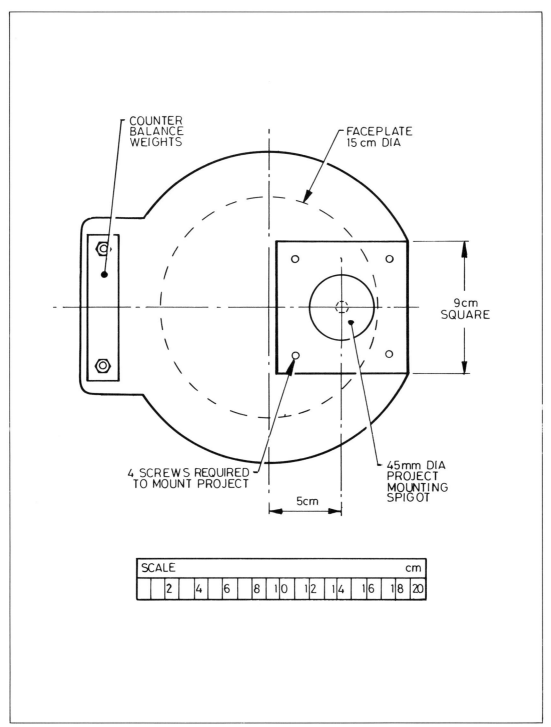

COUNTER
BALANCE
WEIGHTS

FACEPLATE
15 cm DIA

9cm
SQUARE

4 SCREWS REQUIRED
TO MOUNT PROJECT

45mm DIA
PROJECT
MOUNTING
SPIGOT

5cm

SCALE										cm
2	4	6	8	10	12	14	16	18	20

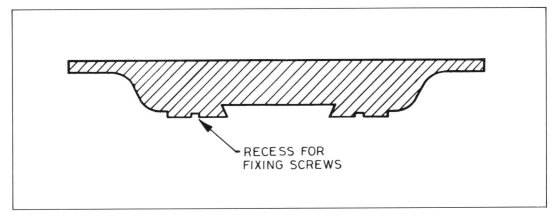

Fig 18.2 Platter blank.

tapped into the new centre of the platter – *see* Fig 18.3. To find the centre, start the lathe and mark the centre with a pencil: when you get a dot rather than a circle, that is the centre. Fig 18.4 shows the jig in use, and Fig 18.5 demonstrates how the black line can be seen when the lathe is switched on.

Grooves

Turn the three grooves out about 2mm deep with the parting tool. Repeat this procedure four times on the different positions for a result like that shown in Fig 18.6. Place the platter back in the spigot chuck and turn out the recess to form the top face of the platter. Finish in the usual way.

Jig 2

The second jig is constructed on a 30cm faceplate; the centre of this jig is moveable and can be fixed in any position along the slots, using bolts and wingnuts – *see* Figs 18.7 and

18.8, also noting the metal strip counterweight balance strips on the right of the photograph. (Almost anything can be used as weights – 18 gauge sheet metal cut up, or 25mm x 6mm x 3mm metal strips, available from tool shops and ironmongers.) The same procedure is used as with the 20cm platter, but this jig can accommodate platters about 30 – 35cm in diameter, and is made from 18mm thick

Fig 18.3 Jig for a felt-tip pen.

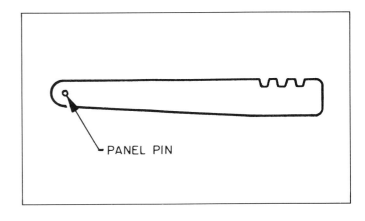

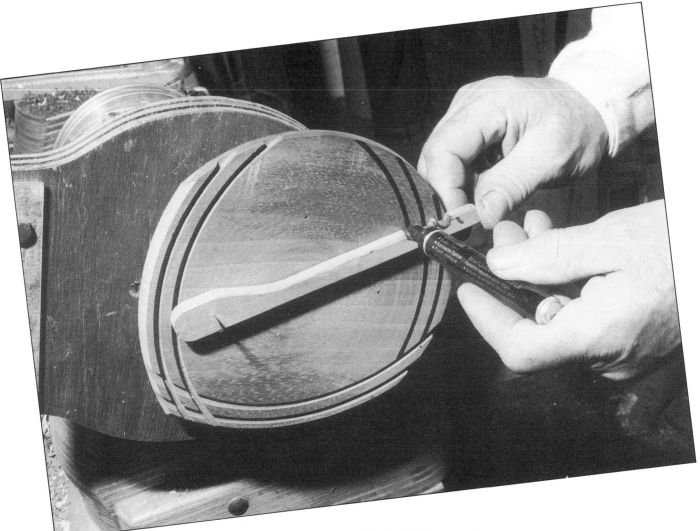

Fig 18.4 Using the felt-tip pen jig.

plywood. There is no moveable block to turn the platter on this jig; instead, the platter has to be removed from the jig to change its position clockwise or anticlockwise, but it can be adjusted backwards or forwards.

To sum up both jigs, the back of the projects are fixed to the jigs with short woodscrews. The holes the screws make in the back of the project can be partly masked by turning a shallow groove with a parting tool where the holes will be made. This can be turned at the time of making the recess for the collet chuck.

Jig 1 can be used to make projects that can be mounted on the jig 5cm off-centre, and can be revolved and fixed in four different positions.

Fig 18.5 Cutting the line.

Jig 2 can be used to make projects that can be mounted on the jig's true centre to 10cm off-centre and can be secured in any position in that range. They can also be revolved and fixed in any position, and can be used to make concentric lines and converging lines.

Both jigs can accept predrilled strips of metal for counterbalance weights.

**Fig 18.6
The platter
with
grooves.**

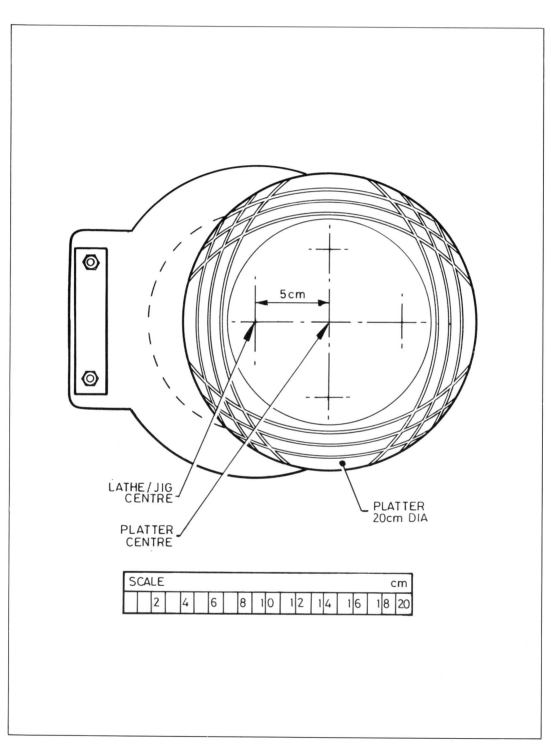

5 cm

LATHE / JIG
CENTRE

PLATTER
CENTRE

PLATTER
20cm DIA

SCALE										cm
	2	4	6	8	10	12	14	16	18	20

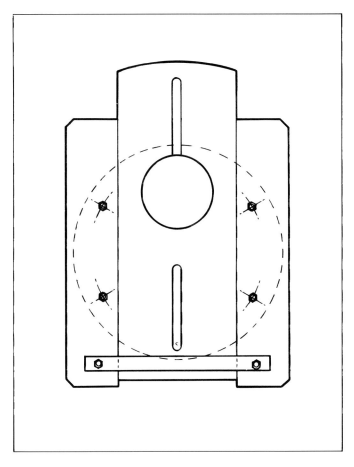

Grooves

The decorative grooves can be turned either as in Fig 18.6, or the centre of the jig can be moved and fixed along the lines of the grooves at, say, 2cm spacings. From Fig 18.8 it can be seen that I numbered the spacing 1, 2 and 3; this was for decoration on a platter incorporating sets of three lines 2cm apart. Each time I revolved the platter on the centre plywood disc and fixed it with woodscrews, I

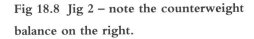

Fig 18.8 Jig 2 – note the counterweight balance on the right.

**Fig 18.7
Jig 2 set up.**

Fig 18.9 Another decorative pattern.

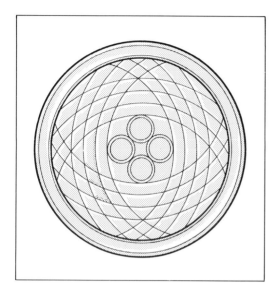

could use the 2cm numbered spacings as a reference to complete the decoration. This will produce a decorative pattern like that shown in Fig 18.10, where the lines on the rim converge.

The platter can be seen on the jig in Fig 18.10.

As an alternative design, the decoration can cover the disc, and the projecting parts of this decoration can be bevelled off with a joiner's chisel and mallet (*see* Figs 18.9 and 18.11); this will give the appearance of woven basketwork. Figs 18.12 and 18.13 show a cheese platter with an offset ceramic tile.

Fig 18.10 Platter mounted on jig 2.

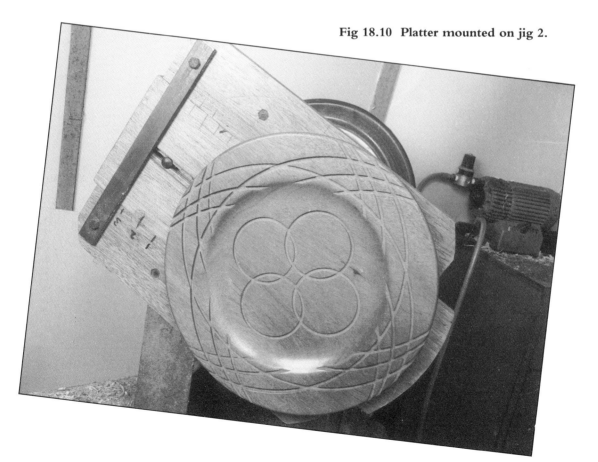

**Fig 18.11
Two finished
platters.**

Fig 18.12 Cheese platter design.

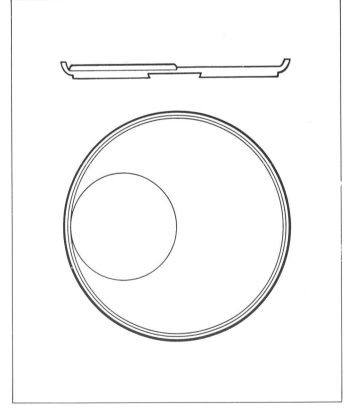

Fig 18.13 Cheese platter ready for use.

Multi-sided Vessels and Platter

The aim of this project is to make multi-sided bowls, with two, three, four and five faces, instead of the usual single-centre round bowls. As with most multi-centre turning, the lathe should be running at a slow speed.

The material needed for the four-sided project will be two 75mm hardwood cubes.

Jig

This project used a 30cm diameter faceplate, and a piece of plywood 30cm in diameter x 18mm will be needed to make the jig.

Mounting a block of wood on the jig to run off-centre on the lathe causes vibration and is dangerous; to avoid this, I mount another similar block off-centre, opposite the first block. The work is then balanced and runs smoothly, and an added bonus is that you will finish up with two bowls.

The aim here is to form a jig on the faceplate that can be revolved into required

fixed positions, and then to repeat this operation on the opposite side of the faceplate to obtain a good balance. As two of the holes in my faceplate were 6cm from the centre, this determined the positions.

The first bowl will have four sides; draw a line through the centre of the plywood disc and mark two points 6cm each side of the centre: these marks will be the centres of two squares to be cut out of the disc. Figs 19.1 and 19.2 show the positions of the moveable bowl jigs for three- and five-sided vessels.

Having cut out two 8cm squares, screw the disc on to the faceplate, then cut two more squares from another piece of plywood to fit neatly into the square holes. These squares should be fixed through the faceplate with hex-headed bolts, sunk flush into the centres of the squares and then held in position through the faceplate with wingnuts. Now cut two 3mm plywood discs 45mm in diameter; these discs

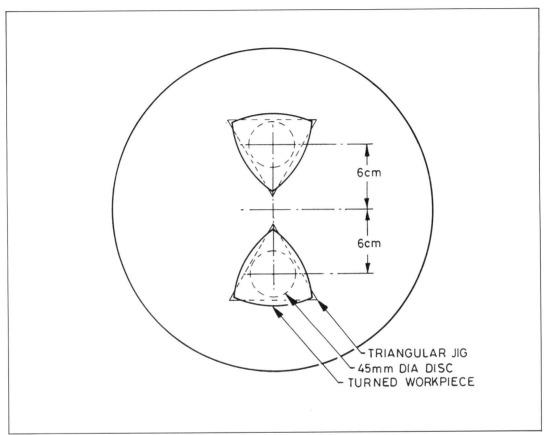

6cm

6cm

└ TRIANGULAR JIG
└ 45mm DIA DISC
└ TURNED WORKPIECE

**Fig 19.1
Moveable
bowl jig.**

can be glued centrally on to the 8cm squares.

Method

First take one of the 75mm cubes and drill a hole central in one of the long grain faces to accept a screw chuck. Mount it on the screw chuck and turn a recess to accept a 45mm diameter collet chuck in the opposite long grain face. Repeat this operation with a second 75mm cube.

You now have two recessed cubes to fit over the 45mm diameter discs that you had previously glued to the 8cm plywood squares. Fix the two cubes to the plywood squares, with woodscrews passing through the squares into what will be the waste wood section of the cubes.

Now fix the assembled projects into the two off-centre square holes in the jig, using the bolts through the faceplate. The jig should now be balanced; start the lathe at a slow speed, checking that there is no vibration, and start turning the bowls on the outside face to form the bowl shapes, remembering to leave about

**Fig 19.2
Moveable
bowl jig.**

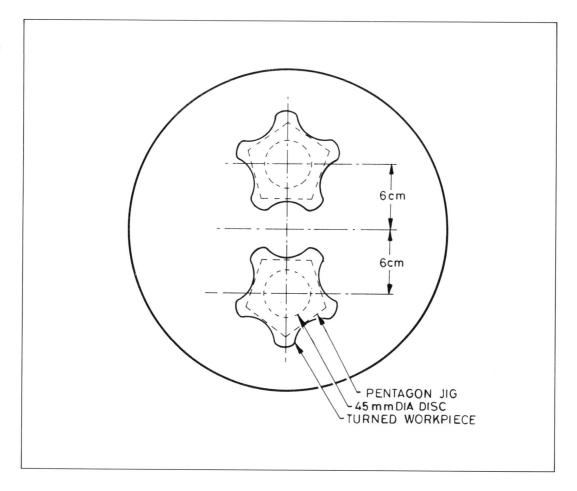

6cm

6cm

PENTAGON JIG
45mm DIA DISC
TURNED WORKPIECE

25mm waste wood at the bottom of the block for later use. The two pieces can be moved to be turned on the opposite faces, and they can then be repositioned to shape the remaining faces, to form a four-sided project. This operation must be performed very carefully; I always wear a pair of industrial gloves, which help save the knuckles.

Remove the blocks from the jig and mount them in turn in the collet chuck. Turn the centre out to a bowl shape, then turn the base

down to form a neat foot and part off with a parting tool, leaving the recess section as waste.

Fig 19.3 shows a triangular bowl mounted on one side of the jig; the other side shows a plywood triangle for this bowl, with the plywood disc ready to receive the second block.

The two three-sided bowls can be turned using the same method and the same-sized blocks. The points of the triangular jigs should be directed towards the centre of the faceplate when setting out, as can be seen in Fig 19.1.

These bowls are turned on the outside diameter of the jig, so one face always will face out.

Although you will only be turning two sides in making the two-sided bowl, the blocks will be mounted on the square jig inserts using the same procedure as for the four-sided bowls.

As the sides need eventually to meet, the material will have to be longer: it will still be 75mm square, but the length should be 170mm. Make the two-sided bowl using the same method as above.

Fig 19.3 Triangular bowl mounted on the jig.

The five-sided bowls set a different problem: if we use the above method, the sides will make the bowl appear almost round. The bowls are turned from the inside or centre of the faceplate to overcome this. This operation is very similar to turning the bites out of the apple in Chapter 11. When the lathe is switched on, it is almost like turning the centre out of a small bowl or goblet; remember, however, that you are not making a small bowl, and keep your hands clear of the work revolving on the faceplate. You will have to be very careful and precise in this part of the project. It is very easy to undo the wingnuts and relocate the bowls for shaping.

For the five-sided or pentagonal bowl, the same basic set-up for a jig will be used as in Fig 19.2; this time the plywood inserts will need to be revolved in five different fixed positions. When setting out the jig, a flat side must face the centre, because we will be turning a central position.

The material for this project needs to be a 10cm cube; while it is mounted on the screw chuck, remember to turn a recess for the collet chuck. Turn the block 9cm cylindrical, turn the cylinder a smaller diameter down towards the base. Glue a piece of foam round a wooden dowel and wrap a piece of sandpaper round it. As you turn each of the five faces, you can sandpaper them without getting your fingers too near the revolving bowl.

When this has been done, remove the bowls from the faceplate, fit them in the collet chuck and finish as before; after sandpapering, give the bowls two coats of Danish oil; liquid paraffin also gives a nice finish.

Platter

You can use the same jig to make a platter for the bowls; this platter can be the same distance off-centre as were the bowls – 6cm. The platter in Fig 19.4 was made from a piece of wood 37cm in diameter x 2cm thick, but if you find it difficult to obtain suitable wood of that size, a smaller platter will serve the same purpose.

Make a platter with a recess to fit a collet chuck about 8cm in diameter, with a wide brim about 4–5cm wide. This will allow room to make the edge of the platter triangular. Cut an equilateral triangle with 10cm long sides from 18mm thick plywood, and make a recess for this through the thickness of the jig used for the bowls. Drill a hole for the bolt you used for the bowls, and then bolt this new triangular section on to the faceplate, using the same centre.

Because the platter is of a large diameter but is still running 6cm off-centre, it will not be too greatly off-balance because some of the weight will be on the opposite side of the centre of the faceplate. Make a 3mm thick plywood disc to fit the recess in the back of the platter and fit this disc centrally on the jig in the same manner as with the bowls.

Mount the platter on the triangular jig using a little glue, or screw it on through the jig. When you have fixed the platter on the lathe, revolve the lathe by hand and mark the design you wish to use with a pencil resting on the toolrest. Release the platter by undoing the wingnut, move it to the next position and continue marking out the design. As part of the platter is mounted over the true centre of the faceplate, you can mark circles that appear to be intersecting, like those shown in Fig 19.4.

When you are satisfied with your design, mark over one of the pencil lines with a black felt-tipped pen. Start the lathe, and make the cut about 2mm deep with a sharp parting tool. The cuts that give the triangular shape to the project should go right through the thickness of the rim. Apply the same finish to the platter as for the bowls (*see* Fig 19.4).

Fig 19.4 Platter and a selection of bowls.

Decorated Bowls

**Fig 20.1
The finished
bowls.**

These bowls are turned on a faceplate, and the decorative work is turned between centres. The bowls' size allows them to be turned between centres on a lathe with a 10cm swing or one that will accommodate 20cm diameter between centres. Fig 20.1 shows the finished project.

A solid sphere 20cm in diameter will be needed: to make a laminated block of wood this size, you will require four pieces 50mm x

75mm x 20cm long, and four pieces 50mm x 150mm x 20cm long. Softwood is fine for this project; pine, even with knots in, will look well with a good finish, and can be purchased already planed all round from most timber merchants. You may even get some offcuts, or you may decide to get enough wood to make two spheres, as it will not be much more effort to true up, glue and clamp together.

Method

Fit the pieces of wood together as in Fig 20.2; they will probably need truing up with a plane first. When they fit together, glue and cramp

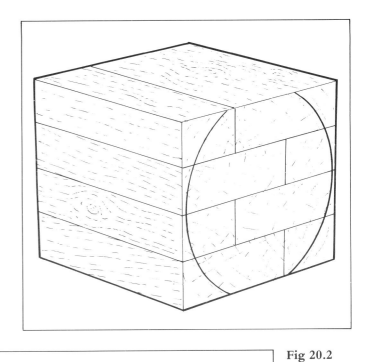

Fig 20.2 Fitting the wood together.

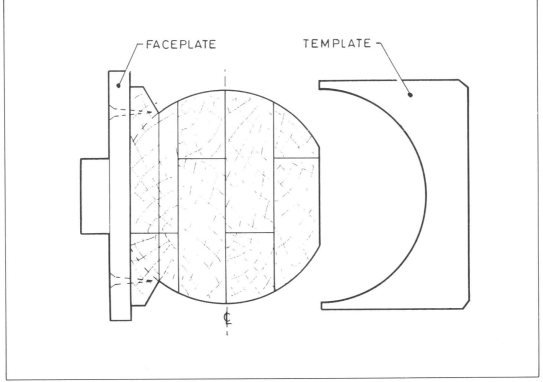

Fig 20.3 Block on faceplate and template.

them to form a square block. The prepared wood you purchase will be undersize, because the sizes given are correct for sawn timber. When this block is turned on a faceplate to make a 20cm sphere, as the thickness of the block will be undersize, there will be two flat areas on it – *see* Figs 20.2 and 20.4.

The flat areas will be useful for this project. First make a half-circular template 20cm in diameter from thin plywood, as in Fig 20.3, and screw the block to a faceplate. As you can see from the line drawings, the centre joint on the block is a centre line for the project. Using the template, turn the block spherical up to where the waste wood is holding the work on the faceplate – *see* Fig 20.3. There will be a flat area left: this will be the bottom of one of the bowls. If the block size is such that you do not have a flat area, you will have to turn one.

Turn a recess in the flat as shown in Fig

20.5, and make a mark in the centre of the recess; this will be used later to mount the sphere between centres. Remove the block from the faceplate and mount it on to a collet chuck. Remove the waste wood; use the template again to finish making the sphere. Cut a recess for the collet chuck as before.

The next part is to mount the sphere between centres to turn the decorative work. The decoration in Fig 20.1 is made up of pairs of beads turned around a sphere; the pattern made as they converge is a bonus. Mount the sphere between centres on the centre line – *see* Fig 20.4 – then spin it by hand to check it is running correctly before setting the lathe to run at a slow speed. It is now ready to turn the first pair of beads – *see* Fig 20.5 for the method of setting out and the sequence of cuts.

The first pair of beads, already formed in the illustration, provides the centres for the

Fig 20.4 Mounting on the centre line.

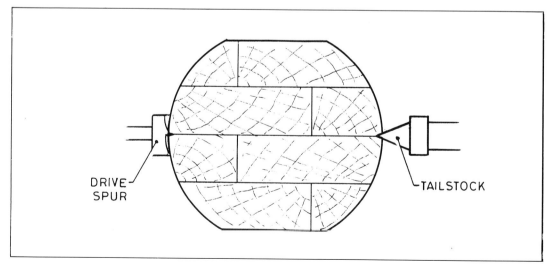

DRIVE SPUR

TAILSTOCK

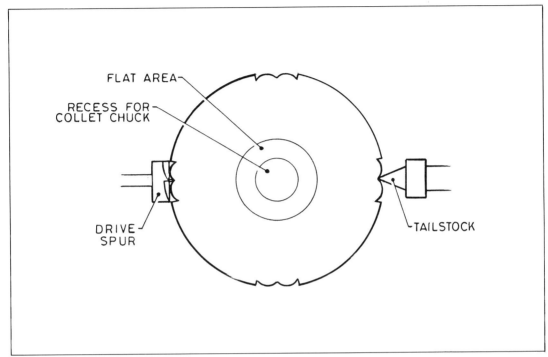

Fig 20.5
Setting out
the beads,
and the
cutting
sequence.

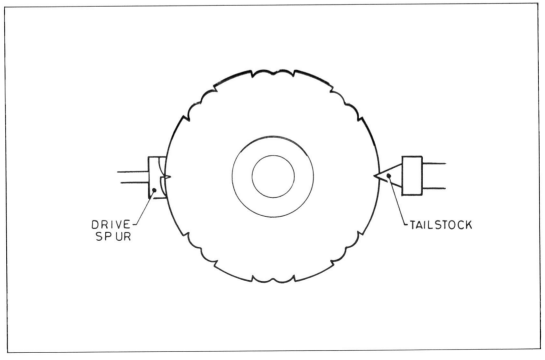

Fig 20.6
Cutting the
third set
of beads.

**Fig 20.7
Two styles
of
decoration.**

second pair at 90°; as each pair of beads is turned, it should be sandpapered and finished. The marks made by the drive spur and tailstock centre will be removed when the sphere is cut in two. The beads work out about 15mm wide on the centre line on this bowl.

We now have a sphere with four pairs of beads at right angles to each other. I do not feel it to be vitally important to make the beads perfectly shaped or exactly the same size on this project, but you should still aim for a good finish. If on completing the project you decide to make the bowl in hardwood, more time and effort on the finish will be needed.

Divide the quarter-circle in two on opposite sides – *see* Fig 20.6, where the third cut is marked. Mount the sphere between centres at 45° to the first set of beads, turn two beads and then remount the wood at the centre of these

beads on the centre line; repeat this for cut four. Use the same procedure to complete the beads round the circumference. When the fourth cut has been made, there will be room for the sphere to be repositioned for the final cuts.

The next operation is to cut the sphere in two: move the sphere from the lathe, fit the collet chuck to the headstock, turn the sphere on to its other axis and mount it between centres on the collet chuck. Now carefully start to cut the sphere in two around the centre line with a parting chisel. Do not cut right through, but finish parting the halves with a handsaw. Turn the centres out of the half-spheres to form two bowls, using a bowl gouge.

Fig 20.7 shows two bowls from the same block, finished in different ways; these are suggested decorations, but the design factor is open for you to use your own artistic talent.

CHAPTER 21

Decorated Orb

Jig

Most of the multi-centre turning projects in this book have only been made once; I have usually gone on to the next idea before repeating a project. I had something completely different in mind for this project, and made a jig from two 30cm diameter x 18mm thick plywood discs with pine wedges between, which gave an angle of 15°, to be mounted on my 30cm diameter faceplate (*see* Fig 21.1 for details of this jig).

It was intended to turn a bowl with an angled bead, and this was achieved, but I also discovered that if, instead of turning the bowl blank out in the usual way and then mounting it at an angle (and all that involved), I could have had nearly an identical result by cutting the foot off and at an angle on a conventional bowl.

The wood used for this project was an unsplit 12cm diameter sycamore branch which I have had for three or four years; I cut two pieces 17cm long from it, and made the two decorated orbs seen in Fig 21.2. The orbs were turned hollow about 4mm thick; although they were fairly dry, there was a possibility of their splitting when brought into the warm, dry atmosphere of the house. The wood may have moved and have slightly changed shape, but the orbs have not split. Any wood 10-12cm square can be used for this project.

Method

Place the material between centres and turn the whole length cylindrical. Slightly undercut the end at the headstock so that the piece will fit firmly on the plywood jig. Turn a 10cm diameter sphere 3cm from the tailstock, as the piece will need to be remounted between centres later and the sphere will also need to be attached by a 3cm diameter stem – *see* Fig 21.1.

You will need a 10cm diameter template made from thin plywood or plastic laminate. As the sphere has to be a true section for this project, the template will have to be less than half a circle to fit over the sphere.

Cut a 20cm diameter disc from 18mm thick plywood and draw a straight line passing through the centre. Square the ends of the lines

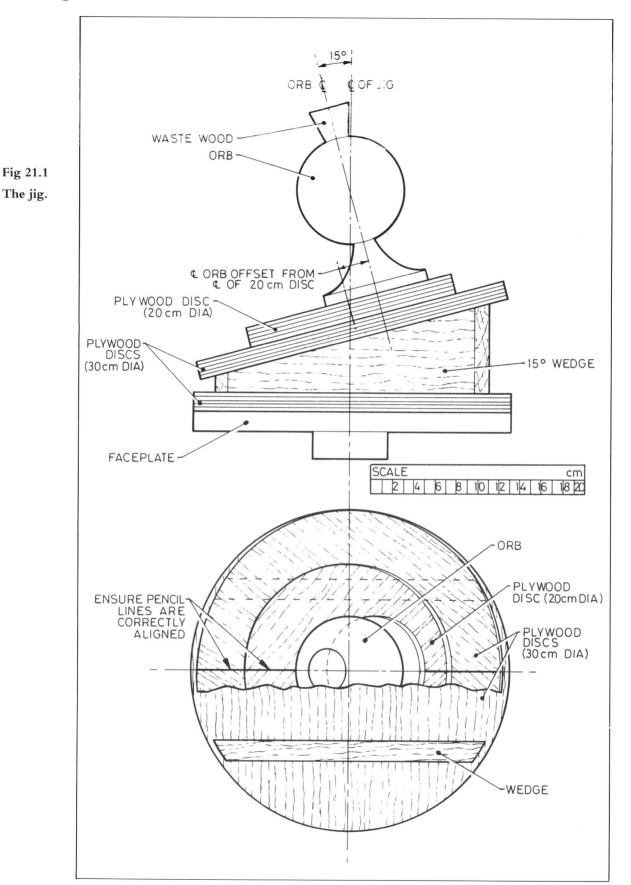

Fig 21.1
The jig.

Fig 21.2 Two styles of decoration.

down the thickness of the disc. Fix with screws through the plywood disc into the waste undercut end of the project.

Mount the angled jig mentioned earlier on to the lathe and draw a straight line from the highest part of the jig to the lowest part, passing through the centre. Place the 20cm diameter disc with the sphere attached to it on to the angle jig, with the line on the disc directly over the line on the jig. The disc has to be moved along the line on the angled jig until the sphere is running dead centre; this will be a trial and error operation: loosely attach the disc to the jig with G-cramps, move the toolrest near the sphere and revolve the jig, tapping the disc with a hammer until the sphere is revolving dead central (*see* Fig 21.1).

When the sphere is dead centre, fit the disc securely to the jig with screws and remove the G-cramps. Fig 21.3 shows the design on the second orb being cut with a parting tool; the orb was moved round 90° in the jig after the first three cuts. Run the lathe at a slow speed, about 1100rpm. The sphere may need some truing up with a gouge.

Make your design, revolve the jig by hand and mark it on the sphere with a pencil resting on the toolrest before cutting. When you have cut the design, finish with sandpaper and remove the workpiece from the jig and remount it between centres.

Turn a spigot on the waste end and place the workpiece in a spigot chuck, then turn off the waste wood used to support the sphere on the tailstock. If you so wish, you can turn the centre out and make a hollow vessel; add a turned lid, and you have a trinket box. I keep all my money in this orb, but remember, there is no such thing as a rich woodturner! Finish with melamine and paste wax, and carefully part off from the spigot chuck.

Fig 21.3 Cutting a groove.

CHAPTER 22

Vases

This project reflects my desire to make use of wood that would usually be discarded; the results obtained can sometimes be very rewarding. In this particular case, 7.5-10cm diameter branches about 30-45cm long are ideal: they may be rescued from firewood or salvaged from damaged trees. The greener they are, the better.

It is not important what wood is used, or even whether you know what the wood is; the surprise results produced can be all the better. I have used such unlikely woods as lilac, hawthorn and poplar. It is usually much easier to turn green wood than seasoned, but of course in log form, the wood will split as it dries out. The splits form along the grain, which helps this project: as the grain swirls, so do the splits. The finished vases can be seen in Fig 22.1.

Preliminary Method

Place the wood between centres and turn to roughly the vase shape shown in Fig 22.2. Drill a 12mm or 15mm hole down the centre, and then open it up to follow the line of the neck.

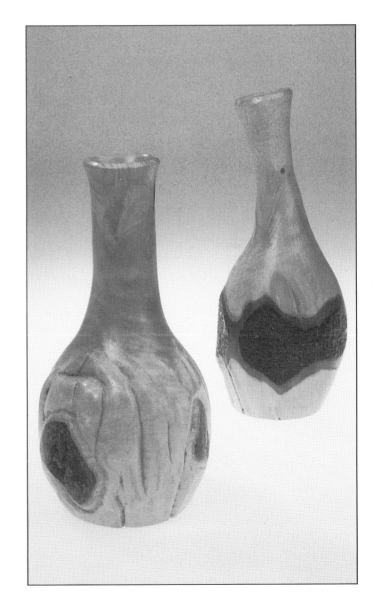

Fig 22.1 Vases turned from green wood.

**Fig 22.2
Vase shape
turned
between
centres.**

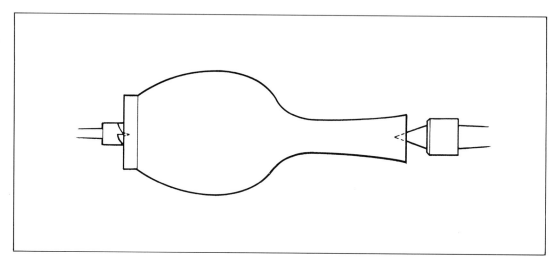

Microwave drying

Now place the wood in a microwave oven to dry out the moisture; this is best done with the oven turned to 'defrost' or 'warm' for five minutes. Take the wood out, let it cool down, and repeat two or three times. The result should be that the base has shrinkage splits; the neck, being hollow, should not have any splits

– it may be distorted and the grain texture may be prominent, but this all adds to the finished project.

Method

Place the vase back in the lathe, with the base in a three-jaw chuck or spigot chuck and the neck supported by a revolving centre, as in Fig

**Fig 22.3
Supporting
the vase
between
centres.**

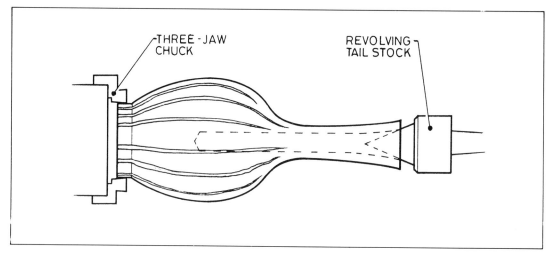

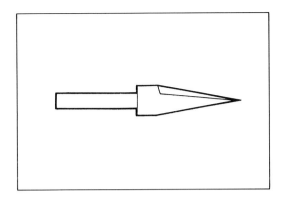

**Fig 22.4
Cutter for
shaping
the splits.**

22.3. Lock or fix the headstock; remove the base from an electric router and, with an acute angled cutter (*see* Fig 22.4), carefully hand-hold the router to shape the splits as A in Fig 22.5. Then do the same with an half-round cutter as B: the idea is to make the wood look thick along the edge of the splits.

Finish off these grooves with 5cm diameter Velcro discs in an electric drill, first with 160 grit and then with 150 grit. Apply sander filler, start the lathe and finish with wax.

If you are satisfied with this part of the project, the multi-centre work can now be attempted; this can avoid a defect or even introduce one if wanted.

First cut a suitable log, visualizing the shape that you can get out of it; cut out the sections not required with a bandsaw to reduce the

**Fig 22.5 Splits shaped with an acute angled
cutter and with an half-round cutter.**

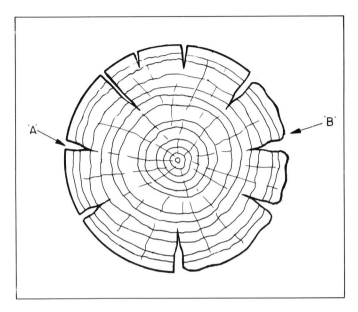

weight, making sure there is enough material left to set the two centres as in Fig 22.6; reducing weight also helps avoid vibration. Partly turn centres AA and partly turn centres BB; drill the hole down the neck, and finish the vase in the same way as described above.

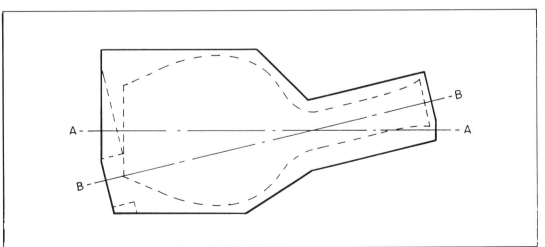

**Fig 22.6
Setting out
the centres.**

Burr Flower in Vase

T his project makes use of a burr and some of the adjoining branch or log; Chapter 31 gives more information about burrs. To start with, it would be advisable to use only 7cm or 10cm burrs; this project used 12cm sycamore burr, and the finished item can be seen in Fig 23.1.

I have developed two methods for turning this project, both of which involve turning between centres and on a faceplate. Low speeds are advisable, about 400rpm on the faceplate and 700rpm between centres; burrs are not normally difficult to turn, as they do not have any long fibrous end grain.

The wood should be turned while still green, and as it dries out in a week or two, a pleasing texture will appear on the burr, rather like a flower.

The burr should be 7–10cm in diameter, with the branch projecting about 15cm or 18cm on either side (*see* Fig 23.2). You will discard the branch on one side of the burr before the project is completed, as it is only needed as a counterbalance to prevent vibration

Fig 23.1 The finished flower and vase.

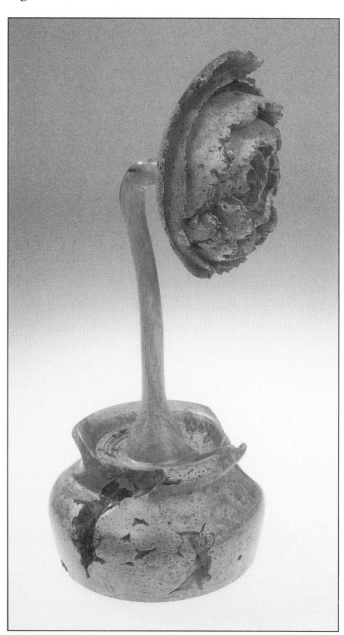

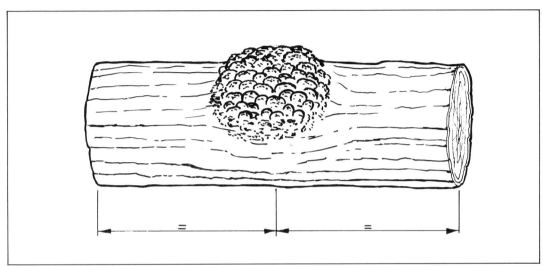

Fig 23.2 Burr and branch.

when the wood is turned on the faceplate, and as a centre for the tailstock when the wood is turned between centres.

Method 1

Cut a section from the back of the workpiece so it will sit flat on a piece of plywood, which in turn will be screwed to the faceplate, with the centre of the burr at the centre of the faceplate. Mount the faceplate on the lathe; the work should now be well balanced, so stand back and start the lathe at a slow speed to check it is running without vibration.

Put your helmet and visor on and, remembering to be aware of the spinning ends of the workpiece, make a hole about 18mm deep in the centre of the burr, using a small spindle gouge or 6mm drill bit.

For the next step I have ground one of my parting chisels, producing a cutting edge similar to that of a skew chisel; this will not harm the parting tool, as it can be ground square again or used as it is for parting off (*see* Fig 23.3). In fact, in some respects it is better in the new shape, as it can be turned over and used either way.

Fig 23.3 Grinding the parting tool.

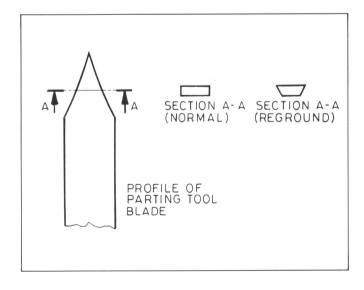

Fig 23.4 Turning the flower on a disc – note the counterweights.

Make a series of incisions with the reground parting tool, as shown in Fig 23.4. At this point you can pick the loose bark off the flower with a bradawl or marking awl; the shape of the flower is then revealed, and the back can be turned in proportion.

Do not remove the waste from the back until all the work has been finished on the front; at this stage the flower can break, as the grain behind the burr can be short and not very strong. A screw through the centre of the flower into the stalk will strengthen the grain; this can be left in permanently.

This whole operation can produce interesting results, so when you frequently remove your helmet and face shield to have a closer look, remember to replace them each time – when absorbed in turning, it is very easy to forget.

The flower can now be finished: a piece of folded sandpaper can be held into the turned recesses, and the back can be sanded – watch your knuckles!

Now select which end of the workpiece is to be the vase, place that end in the drive end of the lathe, and place the other end in the tailstock (*see* Fig 23.5). Before switching on the lathe, revolve the work by hand to ensure the flower does not foul the lathe bed or toolrest: be very careful, as the flower is quite delicate.

Examine the work closely and decide what shape of vase would be suitable, and then turn the vase and stem, leaving the latter to the last and making sure the final diameter is thick

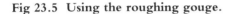

Fig 23.5 Using the roughing gouge.

enough to prevent breakage. It will not be possible to turn the area of the stem behind the flower and the curve of the stem where it joins the flower; this section should be shaped by hand, using a coping saw, rasp and sandpaper. The finishing should be done with two coats of sanding sealer, lightly rubbed with 0000 wire wool.

Method 2

This second method is used when the burr selected is already at the end of a branch, or when there is not enough wood to act as a counterbalance. I was fortunate to find a sycamore branch with two burrs close together, that could both be used for this project: one for the flower, and the other conveniently placed in the branch for the vase or pot (*see* Fig 23.1). The procedure is the same as that given above, except for two operations: one is to place the branch between centres and roughly turn the

vase first to reduce the weight. In the second, as there is only wood at one of the burr, you will need a counterbalance. This can be made by screwing the branch on to a strip of plywood, as shown above; this time, however, the plywood will need to extend beyond the faceplate, to fix counterweights to balance the work.

Fig 23.4 shows strips of metal bolted on to the extreme end of the plywood; these strips can be odd and of varying weights as long as the holes are drilled the same distance apart. Remove the belt from the pulley on the drive shaft of your lathe, which will allow the work to revolve freely; the strips can then be bolted on as a counterbalance. When the work is balanced, run the lathe to check for smoothness. It may look a little disconcerting, but there will not be a problem as long as you **check the mountings are secure and keep clear of the moving parts.**

Jarrah Burr Bowls

I f you buy or are given a section of a burr, the normal tendency is to cut it up into bowl blanks; in doing this, there will be an unused amount of the burr, apart from the wood wasted when the bowls are turned. This is all very sad, when the burr is hardwood and well marked.

For this project, think about the shape, texture and grain of the material you are going to use, and mark out the area to the best advantage with a circular template, which can be made from thin Perspex, with circles scribed at 1cm intervals on it. (This template is also used in Chapter 25.) Fig 24.1 shows a section of jarrah burr marked out to provide two decent-sized bowls; the texture made by a mechanical saw on the face side surface and the projecting burrs on the face edge will be retained.

Method

The burr should be fixed to a jig with counterbalance weights: the jig is an enlargement of the counterweight jig described in Chapter 16. Fix the heaviest part of the burr to the true centre of the jig first, so that you can turn the largest bowl and get rid of some of the weight.

To locate the burr in the correct position on the jig, draw two lines at right angles to

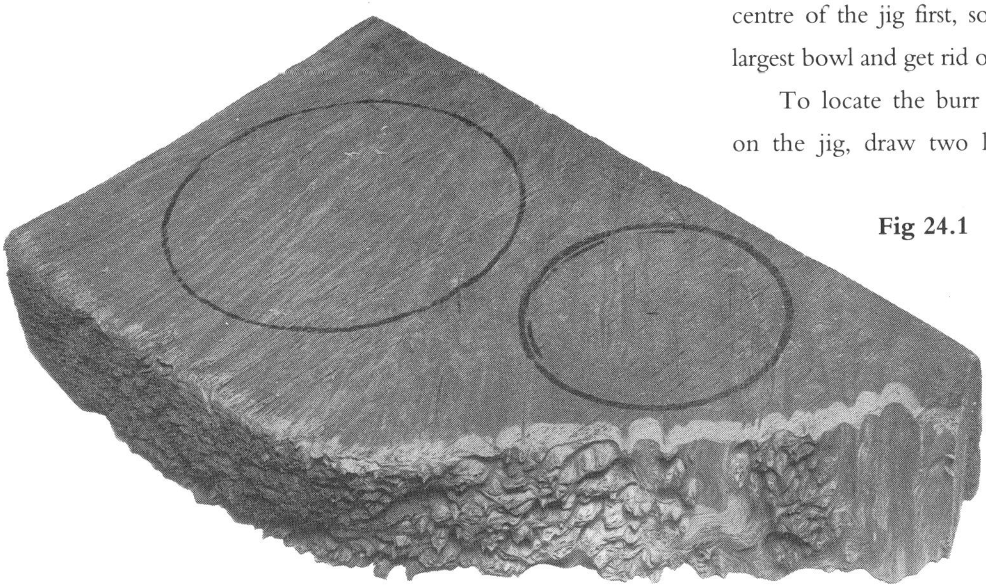

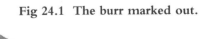

Fig 24.1 The burr marked out.

**Fig 24.2
The burr
fixed to
the jig.**

Fig 24.3 Cleaning the edges – note the fixings through the face corners.

each other on the burr, crossing over the centre of the first bowl. Square the lines down the edges. Now mark two lines at right angles to each other, with the lines crossing in the centre of the jig.

Place the burr on the jig so that the lines correspond, and temporarily hold the burr to the jig with G-cramps. Attach the burr to the jig with screws inserted through the flange of the jig, making sure that the screws are not in the area where the bowl is to be turned. Remove the G-cramps. Fig 24.2 shows the burr attached to the jig: note also the fixings through the face corners, which will be removed later.

Turn the first bowl and finish it completely with the Velcro system (*see* Fig 24.3). Move the burr and centre it for the second bowl; fix, turn and finish this in the same way. Remove the burr from the jig and clean the face side and face edges with a wire brush. Brush two coats of melamine lacquer on these surfaces, as shown in Fig 24.4.

Fig 24.4 The finished bowls.

Chestnut Burr Bowls

I have often noticed how attractive burrs that have been turned into a well-finished vase or platter can be, so imagine my feelings when I was given a big slab of chestnut burr. Not wanting to cut it but wishing to make good use of it, I decided to use the entire flat area by turning more than one bowl from it.

The burr was left attached to the wood, exactly as when it was presented to me.

The construction of the jig used for this project is given in Chapter 16; it was made to fit my 30cm diameter faceplate with a bolt to fit counterbalance weights running through. I then made a Perspex template, which consists of

Fig 25.1 Using a Perspex template for marking out.

**Fig 25.2 The finished bowls,
showing the rim round the largest.**

circular cuts 1cm apart made with a parting tool. The cuts are coloured with different colour felt-tip pens, which helps when selecting diameters. Laying this template on an irregular piece of wood makes setting out and making the most of the material a lot easier (*see* Fig 25.1).

When two bowls had been marked on my burr, there was still an elongated shape left at the end, so I turned an elongated kidney-shaped bowl. The largest bowl was near the centre of the burr; when I turned this bowl, I levelled the rest of the burr with a gouge and scraper, and left a rim standing around the edge of the bowl – *see* Fig 25.2.

Method

Line up the centre of the centre bowl with the centre of the faceplate, and securely fix with screws through the back of the plywood flange on the jig; check that the screws are not placed near where the bowl recess is to be.

Remove the belt from the pulley on the headstock and balance the work, removing or replacing the 25mm nuts on the 18mm bolt as necessary. Revolve by hand to ensure no moving parts foul on anything, then run the lathe at a slow speed and turn out the centre of the bowl in the usual way. Sandpaper with a Velcro disc in an electric drill, seal and completely finish.

Carefully level off the rest of the burr with a roughing gouge and scraper, leaving a flat surface with a rim standing around the edge of the bowl, and then move the burr to the next

bowl centre. Balance the work and again revolve the work by hand before switching the lathe on. The burr will need more clearance now, so more care will be necessary. Turn and finish the bowl as before.

A different method will be required for the kidney-shaped bowl: mark a suitable radius for this elongated bowl on the back of the burr, in this case an 18cm radius (see Fig 25.3), and drill a hole of the same diameter as a number 6 screw 4mm deep at the point from where the radius was marked.

All that is needed to prepare the jig is to partly insert a number 6 screw at a point 18cm off-centre, in line with the counterweight bolt,

Fig 25.3 Marking out the kidney-shaped bowl.

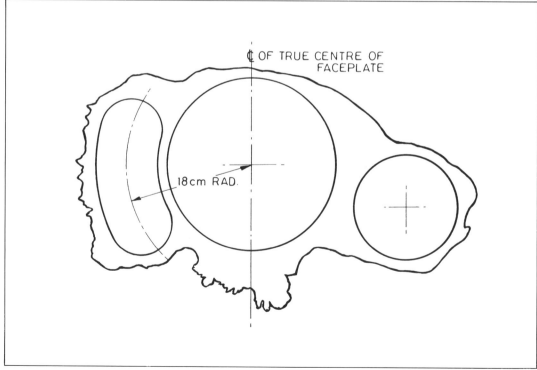

Fig 25.4 Marking out in line with the counterweight bolt.

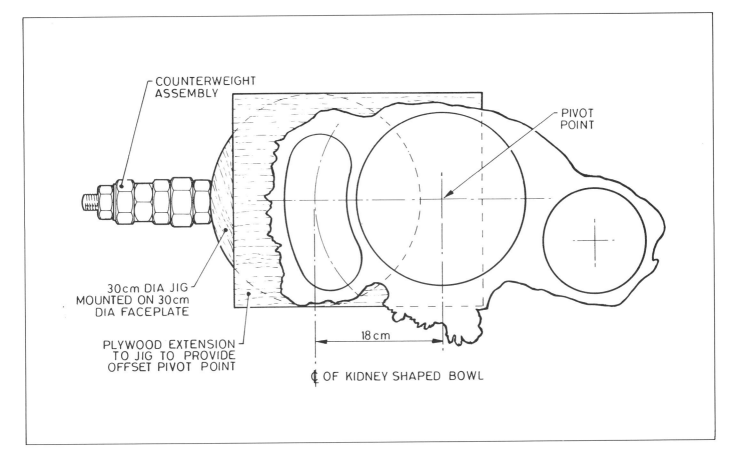

as shown in Fig 25.4. (A photograph of the jig, showing the counterweight bolt, can be seen in Chapter 24.) Cut the head off the screw, leaving a shank projecting 4mm, as shown in Fig 25.4.

Mount the burr on the faceplate, locating the hole in the back of the burr over the projecting screw on the jig. Swivel the burr on the jig until the centre of one end of the proposed elongated hole is over the true centre on the jig. Secure the burr with two screws inserted through the back of the plywood

flange. Revolve the jig to check that the burr is mounted correctly, then insert more screws until it is held securely. Balance the burr, and turn out a bowl section.

Remove the fixing screws, pivot the burr about 3cm on the centre screw and turn out the waste wood. Repeat this operation until you reach the end of the proposed elongated shape. It now only remains to cut off the little waste nibs with a wood chisel. Finish with a Velcro disc and sandpaper, and seal the burr with a melamine polish.

Fig 26.1 The finished project.

CHAPTER 26

Snow Scene

T his idea taxed my concentration more than any other project in this book, yet I feel I have only scratched the surface of this area of woodturning. The contents are a snowman, a large snowball, a fir tree and a bush. Some small snowballs were added later.

Fig 26.2 Turning the recesses.

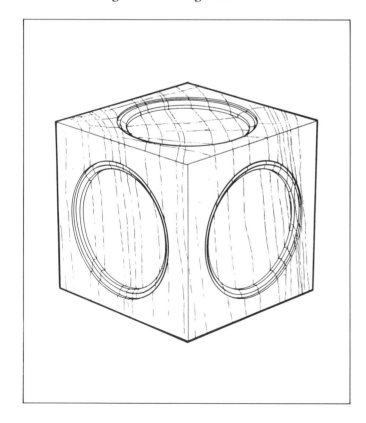

You will need a 5cm x 5cm x 7cm cube of hardwood, a 6mm diameter bar made from small files or silver steel, and 15cm of 18mm diameter electrical conduit tubing.

Method

First study Fig 26.1. Mount the block in a four-jaw chuck and turn a recess 4cm in diameter x 6mm deep on one of the end grain faces. The block can be laid on one side and a similar recess turned; three similar recesses can be turned on the other sides, leaving one face flat – *see* Fig 26.2. As each recess is turned, a decorative bead can be turned on the face edge (*see* Fig 26.3); the five recesses will be the windows for viewing the finished contents, but **all** the turning will be done through the top recess, as shown in Fig 26.3.

Cut some teeth on one end of the steel tube with a hacksaw (*see* Fig 26.4); this tube is used to push in the top of the block to a depth

Fig 26.3 Turning a
decorative bead.

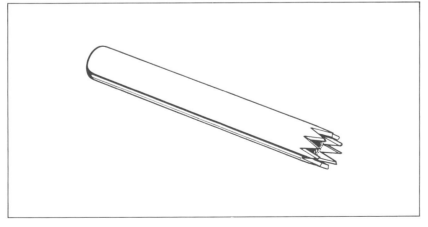

Fig 26.4 Cutting teeth.

**Fig 26.5
Cut away
the waste
wood
(shaded).**

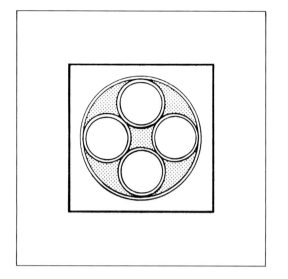

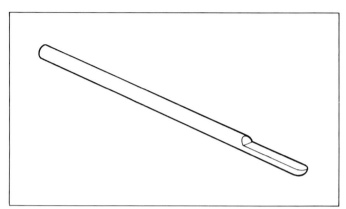

**Fig 26.6
Shaping the
tool for the
snowman.**

**Fig 26.7
Turning
the hat.**

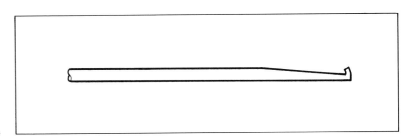

Fig 26.8 Shaping the tool for the hat.

of about 4cm. It is possible to make four such incisions, as shown in Fig 26.5, and the waste wood (shaded in the drawing) can then be cut away with wood chisels and a coping saw. This will leave four dowels standing in the cube: each of the four items will be turned from these dowels.

Remount the cube in the four-jaw chuck and adjust the jaws so the centre of one of dowels is at the centre of the chuck. It is best to make the snowman first: take a small round file or a length of the silver steel, grind one end round and then grind a flat on it, as in Fig 26.6.

Turn the waste wood away from the base of the snowman first; if you leave plenty of wood for the hat, you can tilt the cube in the chuck and turn the hat so that it is tilted on the snowman's head (*see* Fig 26.7). To turn the hat, the tool will need to be reground to form a hook, as shown in Fig 26.8.

Now turn the snowball, regrinding the tool as required. To turn the tree and shrub, first turn to shape; the technique for the final stage is to grind the tool so that, instead of removing a wood shaving, it will peel the wood back but not part it off. Practise this technique on a spare piece of wood mounted between centres first – *see* Fig 26.9.

Fig 26.9 Peeling back the wood for the tree.

Spheres and Caddy Spoons

Spheres

The method for this project is a way of producing near-perfect spheres on a woodturning lathe. The materials can range from wood to Perspex, aluminium, copper, bronze and brass – the photograph in the colour section shows a group of spheres turned in this manner.

The tool used can often be found worn out in a scrap bin; it is a cup-shaped circular cutter or hole saw, used by plumbers and pipe

Fig 27.1 The cutter, before (right) and after grinding.

Fig 27.2 Forming the burr on the cutter – I have removed the industrial gloves to give a clearer view.

fitters for cutting holes in metal water storage tanks and the like, or by electricians for cutting holes in metal trunking. I mostly use a 5cm diameter cutter.

Method for making the tool

To prepare the tool for cutting, first grind the teeth off on a grinding wheel – Fig 27.1 shows the cutter before and after the teeth have been removed. Mount the hole saw in a chuck on the lathe; you will now need a worn or broken piece of grinding disc; should this prove difficult to obtain, an inexpensive 10cm diameter disc for portable angle grinders can be purchased from most tool shops.

Wear a pair of industrial gloves and eye protection for this part of the project.

Remove the centre point from the tailstock, start the lathe and wind the tailstock towards the hole saw in the revolving chuck, with the grinding disc held at right angles to the tailstock. Wind the tailstock to apply gentle pressure – *see* Fig 27.2. – making sure the cutter does not overheat.

Fig 27.3
Turning the
sphere.

You should now have a flat, sharp cutter with a small burr on the inside. It will need a handle; there is a thread in the bottom of the hole saw: if you can find a bolt to fit this thread, turn a wooden handle. You will now have a handle that can be unscrewed and which will fit most other diameters of hole saws.

Method

Turn a piece of wood cylindrical, with a spigot at one end to fit a spigot chuck. (This piece of wood must be a diameter larger than the cutter you intend to use.) Mount the wood in the spigot chuck and turn the end roughly spherical. Remove the toolrest and hold the cutter against the sphere, moving the handle from side to side (*see* Fig 27.3).

The action of the cutter scrapes in the same manner as a woodturning scraper, and the same kind of shaving should be coming off. Any size of hole saw will make a sphere bigger than the diameter of the cup, but do not let it get smaller than the cup, or the cup will slip right over the sphere and may grab the tool. Turn the sphere until it is held on to the waste wood by a small diameter and part the sphere

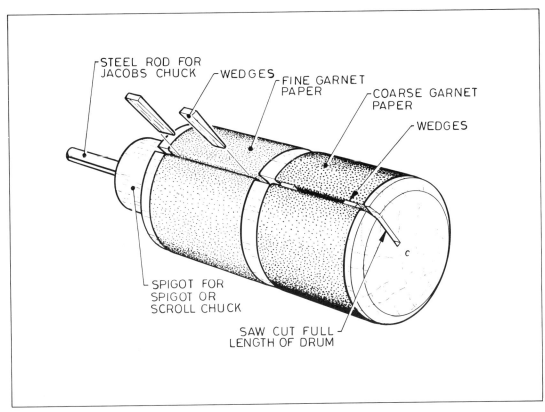

Fig 27.4 Making a drum sander.

STEEL ROD FOR JACOBS CHUCK

WEDGES

FINE GARNET PAPER

COARSE GARNET PAPER

WEDGES

SPIGOT FOR SPIGOT OR SCROLL CHUCK

SAW CUT FULL LENGTH OF DRUM

c

Fig 27.5 Using the drum sander.

Caddy Spoons

Jigs

With a little time and effort, one can usually design or adapt a jig, chuck or template to help on any project; caddy spoons can be produced with the aid of the cutting tool used for making spheres, and you will need a drum sander and a jam-chuck, both of which are easily made on the lathe. Don't be misled by the term 'drum sander'; it is actually a solid cylindrically-shaped piece of wood made to fit in a Jacob's chuck, spigot chuck or scroll chuck, with the other end supported by a revolving tailstock centre – *see* Fig 27.4.

Drum sander

I have no doubt that more sophisticated drum sanders have been designed, but after looking at various sanding systems in DIY stores and noting their limitations, I decided to made my own to suit my requirements. The sanding attachment shown can be fitted with various grades and widths of sandpaper, and I find it useful for general work, as it is only a matter of minutes to change the abrasive paper widths and grades – *see* Fig 27.5.

Garnet paper is best for this attachment; as can be seen in Fig 27.4, the abrasive paper is held in with wedges in a previously made saw

off, leaving a blip on the sphere. This blip can be removed by mounting the sphere in the adjustable cupchuck described in Chapter 12.

When you have had success with making this sphere in wood, try other types of material; I think you will be surprised what a good finish the cutter will make. I have tried making spheres with steel pipes sharpened at one end, without much success; when I decided to use a worn-out hole cutter, I did not realise how successful it would be: the metal, being so hard, keeps its edge for a long time, even when making spheres from non-ferrous metals.

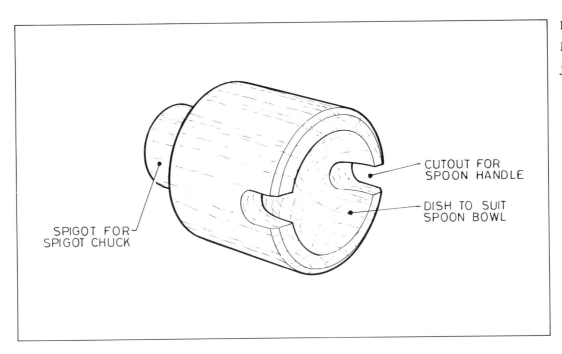

**Fig 27.6
Making the
jam-chuck.**

SPIGOT FOR
SPIGOT CHUCK

CUTOUT FOR
SPOON HANDLE

DISH TO SUIT
SPOON BOWL

cut. The wedges need be no bigger than matchsticks – in fact, matchsticks will do the job. Small wedges are best because, as they are tapped home, the abrasive band tightens on the drum. The projecting ends of the wedges can then be knocked off flush by the tap of a hammer. When the paper is worn out, the wedges can be cut or hooked out with a broken hacksaw blade.

This sanding attachment works well and runs smoothly; there is no trace of bumping, which can be experienced with some sanding belts manufactured with a double thickness where the belt has been joined.

Fig 27.7 A spoon blank in the jam-chuck.

Jam-chuck

The jam-chuck is shown is Fig 27.6; this is simply a block of hardwood turned to a cylindrical shape with a spigot to fit in a spigot chuck, and then dished out to receive the

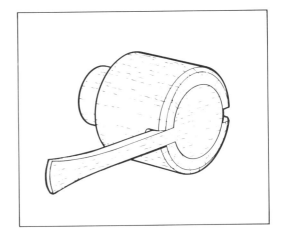

Fig 27.8 Stages of the spoons, and the finished items.

Fig 27.9 Preliminary roughing-out.

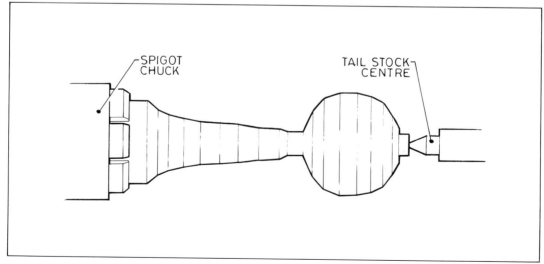

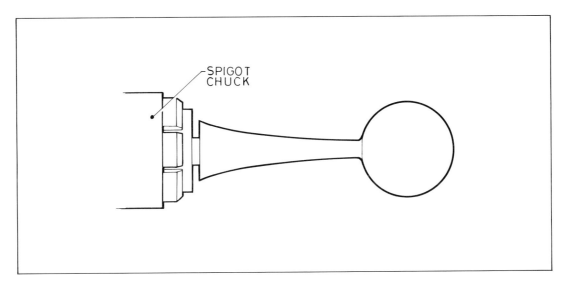

Fig 27.10 Blank in the final stage.

spoon bowl. With this particular jam-chuck, a slot has been cut to accommodate the spoon handle, shown in Fig 27.7. Fig 27.8 shows the caddy spoons mounted in the jam-chuck at various stages, and also the finished spoons.

Method

The material should be 12cm x 50mm square hardwood, turned cylindrical to fit a 50mm diameter spigot chuck. While the wood is secured in the spigot chuck and supported by the tailstock, turn it to the preliminary shape shown in Fig 27.9. Then shape it to the next stage using a 45mm diameter hole cutter (*see* Fig 27.10).

Fig 27.11 Cutting off the waste wood (shaded).

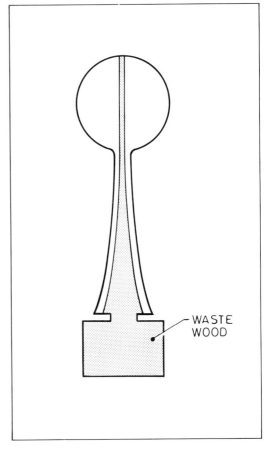

Finish with fine sandpaper and make a cut with a parting tool, also shown in Fig 27.10; leave the waste end on at this stage, so that the blank can be held when cutting on the bandsaw or with a coping saw. Cut down the middle and cut off the waste – *see* Fig 27.11; this will give you two spoon blanks.

Gently tap one of the blanks into the jam-chuck as shown in Fig 27.7, and turn out the spoon with a small spindle gouge, keeping your hands clear of the revolving handle. If you prefer, a hole can be drilled in the blank to indicate the depth to be turned out; this can be drilled on a bench or pillar drill by setting a drill table just over the full depth that the drill will travel (*see* Fig 27.12).

The spoon can now be removed from the jam-chuck and finished on the drum sander; any sharp edges can be removed by fitting a 5cm diameter Velcro pad sanding attachment in the bench drill and holding the spoon in both hands. Should you decide to produce a number of spoons, check the diameter of the sphere on each blank at the stage of Fig 27.10 by offering the jam-chuck up to it. With the help of the hole cutter, it will not be difficult to get a snug fit every time.

Fig 27.12 Drilling a hole to show the depth to be cut out.

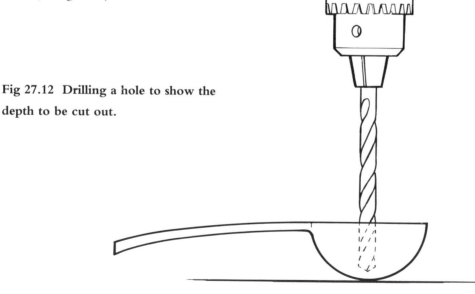

Platter on Signboard

T his project describes the methods used to make my signboard; my logo is crossed turning tools with turned samples of hardwood on a platter. The original platter became warped and damaged, and this prompted me to make a new one; I decided to turn the new platter off-centre on a board, and a piece of

Fig 28.1 The finished signboard – note the crossed turning tools.

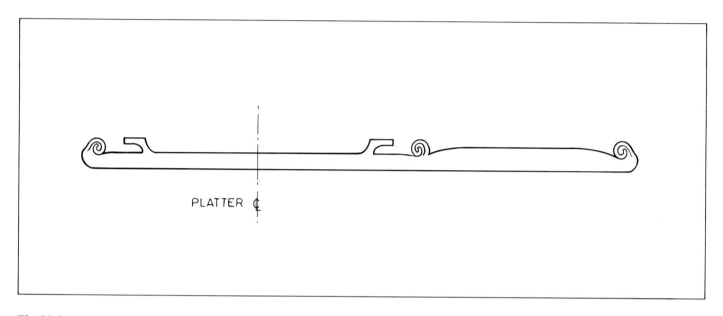

PLATTER ₵

Fig 28.2
Sectional
view.

waney-edged yew (one of my favourite woods) was selected. (A waney-edged board of timber is one which still has the shape of the tree on the edges.) The finished signboard is 90 cm long and is shown in Fig 28.1.

After looking at the shape of the board, the wood grain pattern, the contrasting colours and the sapwood, I selected the size and position of the platter; and to make the best use of this piece, it was also decided to make the ends look rolled over and carved like scrolls. In turning the roll on the end nearest the platter, I found I had an extra scroll on the opposite side of the platter – *see* the section through the length of the board in Fig 28.2.

Method

The yew board was 5 cm thick; to reduce the weight, I scribed an arc from the centre of the

platter to each end of the board and then cut off the waste wood on the bandsaw. The board was then mounted on the 30 cm diameter jig and balanced with the weights on the counterweight bolt. As the turning progressed and the weight of the board was reduced, the weights were adjusted on the bolt to keep a good balance. This was quite a heavy board to turn off-centre in this manner, but by adhering to the safety rules described in Chapter 2, there were no problems or accidents.

When the turning was completed, I carved the ends of the scrolls. Some of the centre of the board had shrinkage splits in it; where these splits cut across the scrolls, I chopped them out and carved new ends on the scrolls. The sapwood had started rotting, too. This board is an example of what can be done with wood that would have ended up as firewood.

CHAPTER 29

Fantasy Bowls

I hope you have found the projects in this book interesting and, if you have made any of them, satisfying. As mentioned before, the methods shown are ideas that can be developed to your own artistic inspirations. This project could be classified as artistic, I thought – but can a specific woodturning piece be given such a title? If not artistic, then this project could be called an unfolding fantasy of mine: one which has generated a lot of publicity as well.

The project is made of cherrywood, and the finished version can be seen in Fig 29.1.

Imagine a single cherry pip on the floor of the forest growing into a mutant cherry fungus. In the bed of the fungus two mutant cherry

Fig 29.1 The realised fantasy bowls.

Fig 29.2 Supporting the stem.

pips are lying together; waves can be seen rippling at the base of the fungus, and a small cherry bowl appears to be unfolding. As it grows its sides stretch outward, causing the ripples to grow, and now the sides reach up, forming a mature bowl.

Well, let's see if we can learn any woodturning techniques from all that.

The material for this project is cherrywood branches ranging from 5-15cm in diameter: green wood can be obtained from a recently pruned or felled tree; a tree surgeon can usually help locate branches. I have used branches that have been cut down for over a year. Because you should retain the bark, check it is still firmly attached to the branch. When the top

layer of cherry bark is peeled off, the underbark looks like leather and can be an attractive feature. When sorting through branches and logs, see if you can find any with unusual markings, or even spalted wood.

Method

Cherry fungus

To make the cherry fungus, start with a branch 12cm long x 5cm in diameter. Mount this between centres; if you mount it about 6mm off-centre at the tailstock end, one side of the finished cone section will be higher than the other – *see* Fig 29.1

Turn a spigot on the drive end to fit a small spigot chuck, or turn a Morse taper end to fit in the headstock. With the branch fitted into the chuck or headstock taper, turn a cone shape in the projecting end of the branch. Finish inside the cone with fine sandpaper, and wind the tailstock into the cone for support. Start to form the outside of the cone, being careful to retain the bark around the top edge.

Form the shape of a cherry pip at the drive end; turn a thin stem and, as it gets thinner, support it with your fingers as shown in Fig 29.2. Finish with fine sandpaper and remove from the lathe, leaving the spigot or taper on for later use. The other two fungus shapes are turned in the same way, the shape developing as the fungus grows.

Bowls

The branch for the first bowl should be about 6cm in diameter x 15cm long. Hold this branch gently in a vice and plane one side flat along the length. Lay the flat section centrally across the faceplate and fix with screws. Now turn the underside of the bowl with a foot to fit in a 25mm spigot chuck; fine sandpaper and finish. Decide what length the wing should be, and cut through with a parting tool.

Mount the foot in a spigot chuck and shape the top section; the outside profile of the bowl should be shaped like a cherry pip with unfolding wings; the spherical shape should be hollowed out through a hole in the top with a

Fig 29.3 Cherry fungus between centres.

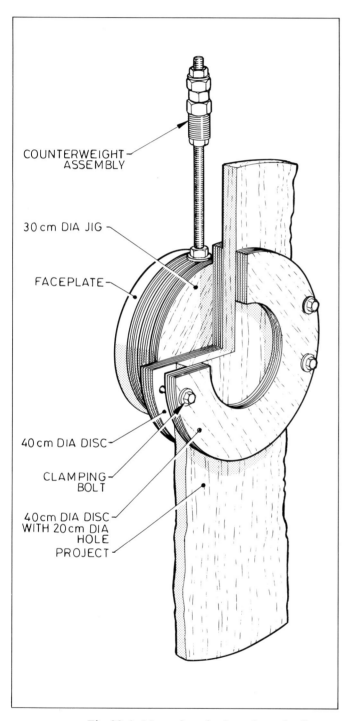

COUNTERWEIGHT
ASSEMBLY

30 cm DIA JIG

FACEPLATE

40 cm DIA DISC

CLAMPING
BOLT

40 cm DIA DISC
WITH 20 cm DIA
HOLE
PROJECT

Fig 29.4 Mounting the board on the jig.

small spindle gouge and should have a smaller diameter than the inside of the bowl section; make the walls reasonably thin and the hole in the top as small as you can. Finish the top, taking care to retain the bark – should a piece fall off, it is not regarded as cheating to stick it back on with a spot of Superglue.

The second bowl is made from a branch 10cm in diameter, and finishes about 7cm long. It is turned in the same way as the first bowl, but the hole in the top is larger and the wings are longer and lift more.

The third bowl is 11cm in diameter, and is turned with a foot to accept the collet chuck. The wings are slightly above horizontal, and the bowl section has a rim around it, as seen in Fig 29.3.

With the fourth bowl, the wings have lifted so that the bark has joined at the ends; the rim has now developed into a complete natural edge.

The final bowl, made from a 15cm diameter branch, is fully developed, with shorter, wider wings; this bowl section is the largest of the bowls.

Plinth and Jig

If you decide to make the cherry board plinth, you will need a clear area of 60cm radius from the centre of the jig; use the 30cm jig with the counterweight bolt through it. Securely screw a 40cm diameter x 18mm plywood disc on the face, then cut a similar disc with a 20cm diameter hole in it and mark out where the

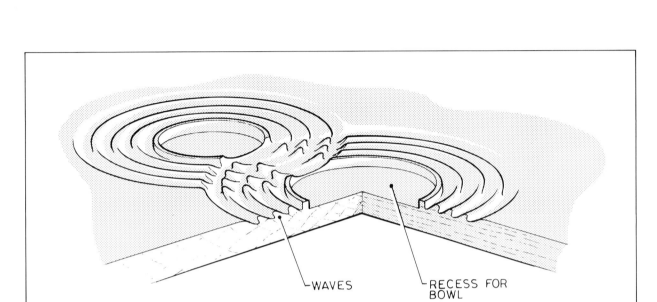

WAVES   RECESS FOR BOWL

Fig 29.5 Turning the waves.

cherry fungus and the bowls are to be positioned on the board.

Mount the board in the jig; fix the ply disc over it and hold this in place with bolts positioned to pass through the discs, clamping the board securely in between, before starting the lathe – *see* Fig 29.4. Again taking all the familiar safety precautions, turn a recess for each bowl and cherry fungus, with the waves around each recess. The waves will overlap and intermingle, and can be simply shaped as shown in Fig 29.5.

If you mount the board dead centre on the jig, a radius can be turned at each end, with a recess to form handles; the section for this is seen in Fig 29.6.

Fig 29.6 Making recesses for handles.

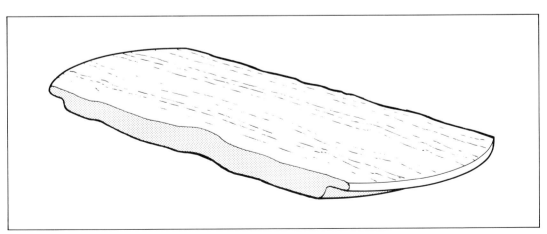

A Family of Multi-terns

Fig 30.1 The finished family.

T his last project is a combination of my love for burrs (*see* the next chapter) and the natural texture of wood, and the off-centre methods already shown in this book. Fig 30.1 shows the finished project. Most kinds of terns have long forked tails, and the other feathers are like streamers. The terns in this project are from a little-known species, and have fan tails.

The base was made from a piece of field maple burr; the burr had grown over a piece of barbed wire, which I found when using my roughing gouge! The wire has been left protruding from the base as a reminder to be observant when using damaged or diseased wood.

Method

Two centres were used to make the base; the burr was mounted on a wedged-shaped block fixed to the faceplate in the way described in Chapter 21. The chestnut branch and burr were turned on three centres: for the inside of the nest, the branch and burr were mounted on the faceplate and supported by blocks of wood screwed to the faceplate and then screwed

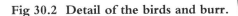
Fig 30.2 Detail of the birds and burr.

through the blocks into the burr.

To turn the two ends of the branch attached to the burr, including the loose ring, each branch end was secured in a scroll chuck, turned at a low speed of about 200rpm, and then parted off, leaving two short waste ends in the chuck.

The two birds were turned using the same method as for the seal in Chapter 9; the off-centre lines were 20° off-centre, which I feel is a safe maximum. The birds were turned by the same method to exactly the same shape, but by cutting the wing profiles on the internal curve on one and the external curve on the other, one bird is looking up and other is looking down (*see* Fig 30.2). I used rotary files fitted into a pillar drill chuck to cut the wing profiles; the finishing used Velcro sanding pads the same way.

The birds' legs, caterpillar, dragonfly body and newly-hatched birds were all made using two centres, the advantage being that, as the pieces were small, I did not have to make jigs for them. The wood was clamped into a three-jaw scroll chuck; to line the centre line of the wood up with the centre of the chuck, I laid a strip of metal 10cm x 25mm x 5mm across two of the jaws. The wood was then placed on the metal strip and secured by the third jaw and a hardwood adjusting block. Where the wood was too thick to do this, I reduced the thickness at the section clamped by the chuck jaws – *see* Fig 30.3. If you own a four-jaw scroll chuck

with independently adjustable jaws, the legs can be mounted as shown in Fig 30.4. The piece of wood shown is larger than would be used, to illustrate the methods; it has an angled section turned totalling 45°, and two lines can be seen marked on the wood.

The wood can be moved in the chuck to the line marked on the section to be turned at right angles to the chuck face. The section of wood furthest away from the chuck must be turned first. If you use this method with smaller pieces than that shown, and take the usual safety precautions, there should be no problems. Once again, this project is the first and only time I have used scroll chucks in this manner, but it shows that new developments are always possible.

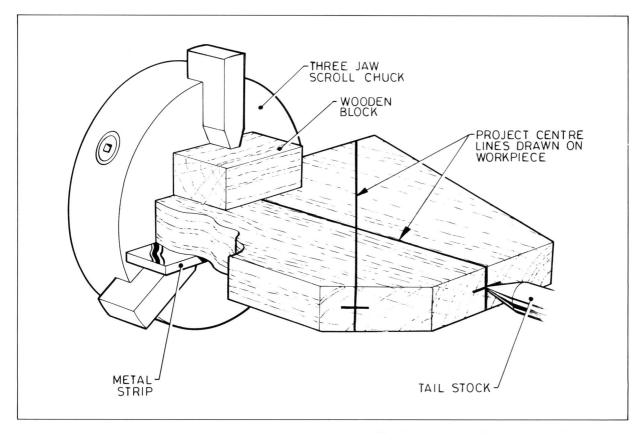

THREE JAW
SCROLL CHUCK

WOODEN
BLOCK

PROJECT CENTRE
LINES DRAWN ON
WORKPIECE

METAL
STRIP

TAIL STOCK

Fig 30.3 Using a three–jaw scroll chuck.

Fig 30.4 Mounting the legs in a four-jaw scroll chuck.

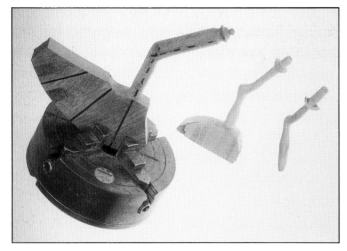

The toadstools were secured by the same method, but the top section was first turned between centres; the bent stem was then turned by clamping the wood in the scroll chuck. The top section and bent stalk were turned in one piece – *see* Fig 30.5.

When you are turning toadstools to mount

on a piece of burr or spalted wood and you would like to make them look a little more authentic, dig the heel of a small skew chisel toward the base when you are turning the stem (*see* Fig 30.6). This is a similar operation to that used when making the Christmas tree in Chapter 26, but it can look as if the toadstool is growing from a small clump of grass.

For the dragonfly's wings, I turned a piece of boxwood to a diameter similar to that of a pencil; this was then secured in the scroll chuck. I then drilled a hole through the centre up to the chuck jaws, using a 3mm drill bit fixed in a tailstock chuck. This gave me a hollow boxwood tube, which I then turned down very thinly. After cutting the tube down

**Fig 30.5 Detail of
the toadstools and insects.**

the middle with a sharp knife, I shaped the two halves to form the wings, which were then glued to the body with Superglue.

The eggshells were shaped by first turning an egg between centres, but in this instance the egg was turned 6mm longer than a normal egg shape. The solid egg was then cut in two, and the halves were hollowed out by being placed into a jamchuck made from a small piece of waste wood. When hollowed, I carefully cut jagged edges 6mm deep to make a broken eggshell.

You may have noticed that the birds' kneecaps appear to be protruding – this is one of the great advantages of designing your own projects: if the kneecaps of this species of bird protrude, that is how it is, and no-one can argue otherwise!

**Fig 30.6
Digging in
with a
skew chisel.**

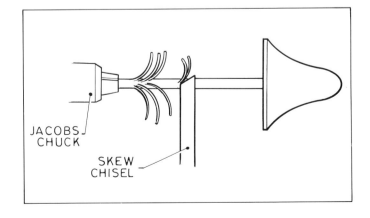

The Burr

The most valued items in my collection of timber are the pieces of wood with burrs on them. (Burrs are known as burls in the USA.) Examples can be seen in Fig 31.1.

There are a number of reasons for this disfiguration forming; as a result of irritation or injury, a virus or fungus can cause a malfunction in growth, resulting in a bunch of small stalks or buds making a contorted, gnarly mass of wood. Once started, these buds keep on multiplying, forming a protrusion.

Do not confuse burrs with crown galls: burrs resemble swollen masses of woody tissue, while the internal cavities of crown galls, caused by bacteria, are lined with dead bark. In the extreme left of Fig 31.1 you can see a chestnut log with a crown gall; I have since turned a 45cm diameter natural-edged bowl from this – it is nothing like a burr, but it makes a good natural-edged bowl.

It is not unusual to see burrs around 45cm in diameter, but they can grow much larger and weigh a few hundredweight; look at the size of the burrs at the base of the tree in Fig 31.2. This 200-year-old oak tree is in the grounds of a friend of mine, who happens to be a tree surgeon and who is keeping this grand old tree alive with care and pruning.

Burrs can range from being uniform in shape to oval and irregular, and some beautiful work can be turned from them; especially good examples come from some of the North American and Australian species. They are usually cut from the side of a standing tree, and the area cut is then treated to avoid further damage. It is rare to see anything other than single bowls, platters and vases turned from burrs. This book illustrates some other ideas.

Fig 31.3 shows my tree surgeon friend using his tractor-driven log-splitting tool to

Fig 31.1

A selection

of burrs.

Fig 31.2 Huge burrs on an old oak tree.

draw a log and split it – a fascinating process to watch. (Note also his protective clothing.) The logs are split into sections ideal for making natural-edged bowls; these burrs are from a field maple, interesting to turn on the lathe and a joy to look at when finished.

The burrs in Fig 31.4 and 31.5 were growing on a rotting sycamore tree, and seemed too good to turn on the lathe. Instead, I levered all the bark off, to expose the true shape of the burr underneath and to reveal the texture of the wood. The largest of these burrs is 35cm high and 54cm in diameter, and weighs 11.7kg (26lb).

Fig 31.3 Drawing and splitting a log.

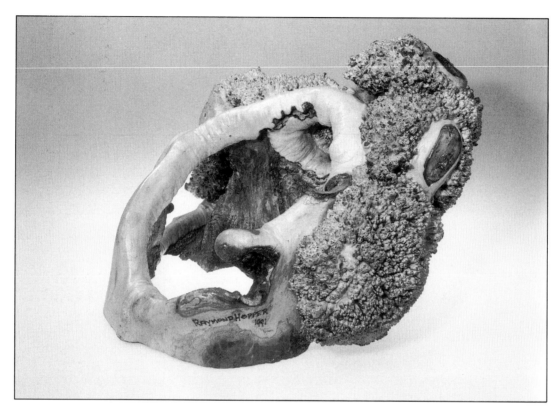

Fig 31.4 Too good to turn
on the lathe.

Fig 31.5 Another burr from
a sycamore tree.

Postscript

By reading this book, you will hopefully have seen that the lathe can offer greater scope than just turning round sections; what I have tried to impart is methods and ideas that can be developed. What I now suggest is that whatever creative or artistic ideas you have, or which may have been sparked off by these projects, that can be expressed by turning wood, should be attempted.

You may be pleasantly surprised. If it does not work out as expected, it will not be a loss: you will have gained experience. Try again.

Metric Conversion

Inches to Millimetres and Centimetres
MM – millimetres   CM – centimetres

Inches	MM	CM	Inches	CM	Inches	CM
⅛	3	0.3	9	22.9	30	76.2
¼	6	0.6	10	25.4	31	78.7
⅜	10	1.0	11	27.9	32	81.3
½	13	1.3	12	30.5	33	83.8
⅝	16	1.6	13	33.0	34	86.4
¾	19	1.9	14	35.6	35	88.9
⅞	22	2.2	15	38.1	36	91.4
1	25	2.5	16	40.6	37	94.0
1¼	32	3.2	17	43.2	38	96.5
1½	38	3.8	18	45.7	39	99.1
1¾	44	4.4	19	48.3	40	101.6
2	51	5.1	20	50.8	41	104.1
2½	64	6.4	21	53.3	42	106.7
3	76	7.6	22	55.9	43	109.2
3½	89	8.9	23	58.4	44	111.8
4	102	10.2	24	61.0	45	114.3
4½	114	11.4	25	63.5	46	116.8
5	127	12.7	26	66.0	47	119.4
6	152	15.2	27	68.6	48	121.9
7	178	17.8	28	71.1	49	124.5
8	203	20.3	29	73.7	50	127.0

About the Author

Ray Hopper left school at 14 to take up an apprenticeship as a printing press engineer, encouraged by his father, but found he was taking out woodworking books from the library, rather than engineering books, and decided he would rather earn a living as a woodworker; he worked at a joiners' shop while studying at the East Ham College of Building for his City and Guilds qualifications in carpentry and joinery, and has since worked in many disciplines of wood (*see* the Introduction). A self-taught woodturner, he is keen to teach and to pass on his knowledge, and has held seminars and classes on multi-centre woodturning in Britain and abroad. He is a member of the Ely Guild of Woodturners, and is married, with two grown-up daughters.

The hat in the photograph was turned from one piece of horse chestnut, and the stick from a cherrywood branch.

TITLES AVAILABLE FROM GMC PUBLICATIONS LTD

BOOKS

Woodworking Plans and Projects	GMC Publications	Making Dolls' House Furniture	Patricia King
40 More Woodworking Plans and Projects	GMC Publications	Making and Modifying Woodworking Tools	Jim Kingshott
Woodworking Crafts Annual	GMC Publications	The Workshop	Jim Kingshott
Woodworkers' Career and Educational Source Book	GMC Publications	Sharpening: The Complete Guide	Jim Kingshott
Woodworkers' Courses & Source Book	GMC Publications	Turning Wooden Toys	Terry Lawrence
Green Woodwork	Mike Abbott	Making Board, Peg and Dice Games	Jeff & Jennie Loader
Making Little Boxes from Wood	John Bennett	The Complete Dolls' House Book	Jean Nisbett
The Incredible Router	Jeremy Broun	Furniture Projects for the Home	Ernest Parrott
Electric Woodwork	Jeremy Broun	Making Money from Woodturning	Ann & Bob Phillips
Woodcarving: A Complete Course	Ron Butterfield	Members' Guide to Marketing	Jack Pigden
Making Fine Furniture: Projects	Tom Darby	Woodcarving Tools and Equipment	Chris Pye
Restoring Rocking Horses	Clive Green & Anthony Dew	Making Tudor Dolls' Houses	Derek Rowbottom
Heraldic Miniature Knights	Peter Greenhill	Making Georgian Dolls' Houses	Derek Rowbottom
Practical Crafts: Seat Weaving	Ricky Holdstock	Making Period Dolls' House Furniture	Derek & Sheila Rowbottom
Multi-centre Woodturning	Ray Hopper	Woodturning: A Foundation Course	Keith Rowley
Complete Woodfinishing	Ian H osker	Turning Miniatures in Wood	John Sainsbury
Woodturning: A Source Book of Shapes	John Hunnex	Pleasure and Profit from Woodturning	Reg Sherwin
Making Shaker Furniture	Barry Jackson	Making Unusual Miniatures	Graham Spalding
Upholstery: A Complete Course	David James	Woodturning Wizardry	David Springett
Upholstery Techniques and Projects	David James	Furniture Projects	Rod Wales
Designing and Making Wooden Toys	Terry Kelly	Decorative Woodcarving	Jeremy Williams

VIDEOS

Dennis White Teaches Woodturning

Part 1	Turning Between Centres
Part 2	Turning Bowls
Part 3	Boxes, Goblets and Screw Threads
Part 4	Novelties and Projects
Part 5	Classic Profiles
Part 6	Twists and Advanced Turning

Jim Kingshott   Sharpening the Professional Way
Ray Gonzalez   Carving a Figure: The Female Form

GMC Publications regularly produces new books and videos on a wide range of woodworking and craft subjects, and an increasing number of specialist magazines, all available on subscription:

MAGAZINES

WOODCARVING   WOODTURNING   BUSINESSMATTERS

All these publications are available through bookshops and newsagents, or may be ordered by post from the publishers at 166 High Street, Lewes, East Sussex BN7 1XU, telephone (0273) 477374, fax (0273) 478606.

Credit card orders are accepted. Please write or phone for the latest information.